# CHOCOLATE PUDDING

## in heaven

### The Intriguing Journey of My Bipolar Mind

MAGGIE NEWCOMB

Chocolate Pudding in Heaven
The Intriguing Journey of My Bipolar Mind
By Maggie Newcomb

1. PSY022030 PSYCHOLOGY / Psychopathology / Bipolar Disorder
2. PSY036000 PSYCHOLOGY / Mental Health
3. BIO017000 BIOGRAPHY & AUTOBIOGRAPHY / Medical

ISBN-10: 1935953699
ISBN-13: 978-1-935953-69-2

Cover Design by Vanessa Perez
Interior design by JETLAUNCH

Printed in the United States of America

Authority Publishing
11230 Gold Express Dr. #310-413
Gold River, CA 95670
800-877-1097
www.AuthorityPublishing.com

# contents

## PART 3 – ADVICE FOR TREATMENT

*This book is dedicated to my family and friends, who have not only accepted me for who I am, but who have tirelessly supported me throughout this journey.*

*A special thanks to Melanie Smith, who was instrumental in guiding my storytelling from the very beginning with her creative advice, insightful research, and wonderful editing of the first drafts.*

# part 1 ∫ PREQUEL

# god's waiting room

I had finally made it. It had been a long haul, but I was finally there. It was only a matter of time before I would cross over. Something amazing was going to happen soon. All the pain, all the suffering, all the struggle would end. I was about to start a brand new life. A fresh start, free from illness or worry or the devastation of failure. Free from loneliness, poverty, or sadness. The excitement and curiosity filled my body, but somehow I felt calm and at peace. This was the feeling that I'd heard about. They were right! The metaphysical authors, the gurus, the mystics, they were all right! I felt incredible. I was about to go to a new world, a new dimension. I was about to go to heaven, and when I did, I would begin to live a new life. I was so close.

I felt sorry for those around me. They would have to stay here. In a world where time and money controls every aspect of life. Where everyone is playing a role, so focused on what they're supposed to be doing. They are obsessed with technology and social media. Their eyes are closed to the miracles around them. They struggle and push every day just to survive. I was done with that dreary existence.

I was in what I could only guess to be heaven's waiting room, or what I would call God's Waiting Room. Not as glamorous as I would have thought, but after what I had been through, I didn't care. The backdrop didn't matter. It was just a portal. A temporary holding place.

My eyes took in the environment. It was a spacious room, kind of like a community center. This large airy room had a sliding glass door that led to the patio and a garden. In the main section of the room, closest to the patio sat a large television and a couple of couches. Near the couches stood several tables, one long one and a few small ones. On the other side of the room near the entrance was a small table against the wall that held a pitcher of water and a pot of coffee. The floors were white and so were the walls.

The light from the outside garden bathed the space with incredible brightness. The temperature was perfect, neither cold nor hot. Very comfortable. The room was spotless, with a slight smell of Pine-Sol. The sliding glass door to the garden was open, allowing the fresh air to fill the room. The patio and garden area was about the size of a residential backyard. The patio's concrete slab, with a table and umbrella, was surrounded by lush green grass. Colorful flowers bordered the grass, and shrubbery with vibrant green leaves lined the edges. When I stared at the flowers I saw a few orange and purple birds of paradise around the palm trees. *Birds of paradise,* I thought. Huh. How appropriate.

I sat at one of the tables facing the sliding glass door to the patio and garden. My shoulder-length, wavy blonde hair was down. I rarely ever wore it down, as it was normally frizzy and out of control. But there it was, tame and beautiful, the curly locks resting on my back. I wore olive green cargo pants that fit my body perfectly. At six-feet tall it was always hard to find pants that fit, yet there they were, just long enough. I wore a tight black tank top with a light blue, button-up sweater.

I sipped my coffee as I sat there in peace. In the transitional world in which I waited, food and drink were not necessary. It was comforting to sip on something, a taste that felt like an old friend. A general calm pervaded the room. There were a few people there, resting on the couches or sitting outside. I didn't think that they'd be going where I was going, but on closer inspection, maybe they were. It seemed that, like me, they were *different*. Like me, they were misunderstood and didn't belong in this world. Yes, now I could see that they were on a journey as well. They could feel things on a deeper level, like me. And at this point, none of us needed to do or say anything. Everything in our lives had already been done.

For the first time in my life, I had nowhere to go and nothing to do. There were no deadlines, no appointments, no meetings, nothing at all that I was supposed to be doing. No alarms, no phone calls, no responsibilities. All that was required was to relax and wait. I would be taking nothing with me. I didn't need anything where I was going. I had no need for possessions, and that was fine with me.

An attractive young African-American man in his early twenties sat on one of the couches reading a *Sports Illustrated*. He smiled faintly as he flipped through the pages. He had such a gentle and kind spirit that I felt at ease near him. There was also a young girl that sat on the patio looking out into the garden. She seemed to be taking it all in as well. She had sandy blonde, curly hair with light freckles sprinkled on her face. Her simple innocence was appealing. A charming older woman, her arms encircling her purse, sat in one of the chairs. She caught my eye and smiled. She reminded me of Sophia, the oldest of the four female characters in the sitcom *The Golden Girls*.

I looked down at the table. I had a fresh, clean piece of paper and a nice, shiny new pen. I finally was able to write. I had wanted to write for a long, long while, but life had always gotten in the way. Now was my time to get all of my feelings out. My brain was pulsing with a profusion of interesting thoughts! Philosophy, spirituality, religion—I was bursting with ideas. Better yet, I was now beginning to understand everything. I was like Einstein, with the secrets of the universe there at my fingertips. I couldn't wait to start putting all of my thoughts on paper. The insights and revelations that were playing through my mind were indescribably exhilarating.

It was a far greater than any "Aha" moment. All these concepts that for so long had seemed so dense now seemed so simple. And wherever it was that I was going, I was going as a better person. I was, as I sat there in God's Waiting Room, the very best version of myself. And, happily, I knew that where I was going I would finally be able to share these ideas with others.

The people who worked here, however, were absolutely clueless. They had no idea what was about to happen to me. One of them walked up to me, holding a clipboard.

"Excuse me," she said. She was a stoic, smaller woman in her mid-thirties.

"Yes?" I replied.

Then she asked, without any emotion, "Have you heard any voices or had any hallucinations in the last hour?"

"Um, no," I replied.

"Okay," she said, and wrote something down on the clipboard. She tried to smile, but it didn't really work. Then she walked away.

Okay, now I know what you're thinking. This place sounds less like heaven's waiting room and more like a mental hospital. Well, you might have a point. Okay, you're partially right. Okay, okay—you're completely right.

Technically, I was in a mental hospital. Or at least the part of me that was my body was in a mental hospital. But my mind, my thoughts, my soul—whatever you want to call the part of me that's more than the part that was sipping coffee at the table—was not. I truly believed that I was experiencing a form of enlightenment, and that I was stepping into a different dimension. I thought that this new realm of existence was heaven or at the very least a totally new life in which I would have spectacularly cool powers. I was sure something amazing was about to happen. But I was aware of what my family and friends thought about what I believed.

I knew that they thought I was having another manic episode, similar to the one I'd had ten years earlier at the age of sixteen. At first I'd thought that this might be an episode as well. However, the evidence to the contrary over the last few weeks had been overwhelming. All the signs, the many, many signs, were so graphic, so palpable, so *real.* The metaphors, the secret messages and the coincidences were everywhere. I had tried, really tried, to ignore them, but eventually I had to give. More importantly, the feelings that had accompanied the signs and events were just as powerful. They were strong and visceral, and on the wave of these powerful feelings I had been led to profound spiritual and philosophical insights. I was at the level of awareness that could help unlock the secrets of the universe, and it was tremendous.

These realizations were very similar to those that I'd had at sixteen. When I tried to share those revelations with those around me, I did not get the reaction I was expecting. I kept trying to share what was, to me, a rare and exciting experience, but to those around me I sounded crazy. They wanted to help me but they couldn't understand what I was saying. Consequently, I was put into a hospital and diagnosed with a mental illness.

I now realized that they had made a big mistake. I was not mentally ill; I'd just never gotten to complete my journey. I let the world around me convince me that I was sick. Not this time. I was an adult: I knew I was neither sick nor ill. I was powerful beyond my wildest dreams, and was about to enter into a magical realm full of possibilities.

Just like the last time, I tried hard to explain what I was experiencing to my family and friends so they could join me, so they could be a part of this fantastic voyage. But no matter how I put it, no matter what way I tried to describe it, I couldn't accurately put into words what I was seeing and feeling in a way they could understand. They didn't get it. And after a while, I didn't care. I didn't need them. I just wanted them to leave me alone so I could begin my journey to a new life.

Even though I was aware that I was in what people referred to as a mental hospital, it didn't matter. I was with my people, and I was at peace. We were all crossing a threshold, and I knew deep in my heart that my life was about to change into something wondrous, something extraordinary. I would be taken to a place that was free of pain and full of love and joy.

Although I had been experiencing mind-blowing coincidences and insights for weeks, the awareness of where I was headed had crystallized in the past several days. Just a few short weeks earlier I had led a "normal" life with an annoying full-time job and zero delusions of my life changing. Who said miracles couldn't happen?

Little did I know that what I was experiencing was just the beginning of another type of journey, one that would prove to be astonishing, painful, exhilarating, and wholly unbelievable. However, at that moment I was in God's Waiting Room, and I was safe.

Lucky for me, the chocolate pudding in God's Waiting Room was quite amazing.

# scared to come out

I can't begin to tell you how scared I am to publish this book and put my story out there. I wonder if people will look at me differently. I fear that it could ruin my life, the life I have worked so hard to create.

If you met me you wouldn't think I was different. Just like anyone else, I go to work every day and come home to relax at night. I DVR educational programs like *Nova* with high intentions of watching them, but I usually end up watching horrible reality shows like *The Real Housewives of Orange County.* With the curtains closed, of course. I go to Trader Joe's for most of my groceries. I usually lament to the cashier that I left my environmentally considerate cloth bags in the car, but I am too lazy to go get them. I work out at a gym, regularlyish. I watch cat videos on my lunch break. My phone is several versions behind the current trend. I spend way too much money on haircuts and skincare products. I relish a great find from Ross or TJ Maxx.

I am fairly well-educated, with a master's degree in Adult Education, but about twice a year I feel like I have no practical skills and wish I were a veterinarian. I mean if there were a zombie apocalypse, what value would I have? I guess if you needed someone to determine if the zombies were visual, auditory or kinesthetic learners I would be useful. Other than that, I don't have much to offer a post-apocalyptic society and would probably be the first to be eaten.

Despite my full if somewhat ordinary (non-zombie) life I have created, I feel like I have this secret. I have been living a lie for over two decades. It's kind of like those Russian spies who pretend to be Americans for years and then resurface. Okay, my secret isn't as cool as the ones you hear about with Russian espionage. I have been secretly living with a serious mental illness for the past twenty years.

*Mental illness* is an incredibly uncomfortable term. The entire topic is misunderstood. We all know it exists, but nobody talks about it. That reminds me of when you're watching a movie with your parents and a sex scene comes on. You feel weird and your parents feel weird, but no one will acknowledge the elephant in the room. You all sit there in silence, hoping it will be over soon. Man, that is uncomfortable. I think that's the way our society deals with mental illness. We don't talk about it and we wish it would just go away.

If people do talk about mental illness, it's usually in a very negative context. It's often whispered about in private. You may hear about someone's cousin who committed suicide or Great Aunt So-and-so who had mental problems. It's usually tragic, sad, permanent and very far removed from our own lives. Mental illness seems to pertain only to "other" people, not us. Nobody that is "normal" has a mental illness.

Actually, that isn't the case. According to the National Institute for Mental Health, "An estimated 26.2 percent of Americans ages 18 and older, or about *one in four adults,* suffer from a diagnosable mental disorder in a given year." A quarter of our population is dealing with a mental illness, but nobody will talk about it. It is not far removed from us, it IS us. There isn't just one elephant in the room; there are millions of them! And they are everywhere. Mental illness doesn't just affect the homeless or drug addicts. It affects everyone: our family members, our friends, our neighbors. Everyone.

And what does that term *mental illness* really mean, anyway? We often use the term "crazy" when we refer to someone with a mental illness. In my opinion, we all have our crazy moments in life, making the line between having a mental illness and not having one very gray. It is a mental illness when those (for a lack of a better term) "crazy" moments start to interfere in someone's daily life. According to the National Alliance on Mental Illness (NAMI), mental illness is a medical condition that doesn't just affect a person's thinking, feeling, and mood; it also completely disrupts his or her daily functioning. For example, everyone gets depressed now and again, but if you can't get out of bed for several days, there may be more going on than just ordinary mood swings. Many of us have anxious moments and have turned our cars around to double-check that the garage door is closed, but you know it may be an issue when you're late for work and you are going back for the third time to check.

New research is coming out that mental illness isn't a mental or behavior disorder at all but an actual brain disorder. This theory was introduced in a lecture by Thomas Insel, M.D, the director of the National Institute of Mental Health. In my opinion this theory takes the mystery out of mental illness. Rather than being a personality problem, it's an issue with the neurons firing in the brain. Unfortunately these theories are not completely developed, and we may have a long way to go before this will have a major impact on treatment.

The term mental illness can also be confusing because it is used to describe a wide range of illnesses. There are a lot out there. Some of the major and more serious ones that the National Alliance on Mental Illness (NAMI) lists include major depression, schizophrenia, bipolar disorder, obsessive-compulsive disorder (OCD), panic disorder, posttraumatic stress disorder (PTSD) and borderline personality disorder. Mental illness can mean a lot of different things.

Scores of celebrities throughout the ages who were known to be "crazy" or "mad" are now believed to have had a diagnosable mental illness. Some examples are Ludwig Van Beethoven (bipolar disorder), Charles Dickens (depression), Howard Hughes (obsessive compulsive disorder), Vincent van Gogh (bipolar disorder), Virginia Woolf (bipolar disorder), Ernest Hemingway (depression), and Winston Churchill (bipolar disorder), to name a few. Some of these cases were more extreme than others. Some were able to live productive lives, but for many of them, their lives ended in tragedy.

Despite the number of people mental illness affects in this country, the subject is still enveloped in extreme ignorance and debilitating stigma. In this modern, technologically advanced society, mental illness is still taboo. It's certainly not the topic of everyday conversation. There are still people and organizations that say that mental illness doesn't even exist (Psst! Tom Cruise, I am talking to you.) Our country has advanced in many ways, but when it comes to mental illness we are still in the age of chainmail armor and the quill pen.

The continuing confusion and powerful stigma attached to mental illness regularly stops people from getting help. We see the effects everywhere: people commit suicide, overdose on drugs. They have mental breakdowns and they don't come back. Those with mental illness that you most often hear about are the ones that haven't found a way to treat the illness. This may be because many assume mental illness is not treatable. However, with advances in medications and therapy, mental illness can be treated, allowing people to live normal lives. I know this because I am someone who has found treatment that works for me.

At first, I tried to be forthcoming about my story. But whenever I would mention my experience with mental illness—bipolar I disorder with a splash of anxiety disorder, to be exact—it made people very uncomfortable. Therefore I developed the "don't ask, don't tell" policy that I have been living by for years. Although not particularly effective for the military, it has worked well for me. I did this because I want to be here, I want to be a part of the world. With a diagnosis of bipolar disorder, a mental illness, it feels like the world doesn't always want me.

In my experience, mental illness shares a distinct similarity with drug use: whether you have a good trip or a bad trip, you still have to deal with the hardship of returning. However, mental illness and drug use differ in a big way, too: when people are on drugs, we recognize that the drugs make them act that way, not the person. We can separate the two. When people have a mental illness, they *are* the illness. I am afraid that if I share the secret of my mental illness experiences, people won't be able to separate me from my illness. I could lose credibility.

So, this is the first time I have ever allowed myself to talk candidly about what I went through. Even many of my close friends don't really know. When I had my three episodes of bipolar mania, it really scared those closest to me. They felt like they had lost Maggie, the Maggie that they knew and loved. So, over the years we rarely talk about what happened. That made it easier for me to just remain silent. Why force my loved ones to relive what I myself didn't want to reencounter?

With this inability to share my story these past 21 years, I often felt very alone. I have never really seen a person with mental illness that I can relate to, even on television and in the movies. Let's face it, most Americans are influenced, if not educated, by what they see on the television and in the movies. Myself included. The majority of media narratives make their characters with mental illness so grandiose, extreme or completely dismissible. Usually they're geniuses, murderers or vagrants. There isn't much in between. It's either Russell Crowe in *Beautiful Mind,* Kevin Spacey in *Seven* or the forgettable babbling homeless person that we see in so many movies and TV shows.

Sometimes I wish my bipolar life were a little more exciting. Although when I was manic, I did tip a Denny's waitress $50 on a $6 breakfast. Nonetheless, from the outside I may seem like a very boring manic-depressive. However, if you read my story, that is the farthest thing from the truth. I am a rare specimen of humanity: I lost my mind and have come back to tell about it. At times it was a wonderful dream, full of beautiful and breathtaking feelings, and at times it was a nightmare, full of hellish anxiety and pain.

In addition to sharing my story, I want to emphasize this: I am *not* defining bipolar disorder. Mental illness manifests differently with each person. Please keep in mind as you are reading this book that bipolar disorder on me can be very different, can look very different, than it does on you, or on someone you love. There are many others out there living with bipolar disorder. Although we may have similar symptoms from the illness, we are all very diverse and have our own stories.

Not all those living with bipolar disorder will have the same experiences as me. Furthermore, not everyone living with bipolar disorder will encounter psychosis—let alone thinking they are going to heaven. My journey is just one example of how this illness can manifest and be treated. In addition, please know that professional treatment, especially medication, affects everyone differently. I will discuss the medications that I have taken, but not everyone will have the same reactions to them as I did.

Unfortunately, trying to articulate what happened during my episodes is extremely challenging. It's like trying to describe a dream. You know that feeling when you just wake up from a really, *really* intense dream? It could have been blissfully good or horribly bad, or maybe a little of both. Maybe a half-eaten zombie is chasing you. You are running for your life and you wake up in a cold sweat. Or maybe you're about to kiss Leonardo DiCaprio or Sandra Bullock, and you are filled with excitement. The feelings are *so* real and *so* powerful.

One of the first things you want to do is share your dream with someone, your spouse, roommate or co-worker, perhaps. But as soon as you try to put it in words, it doesn't make sense. You can't seem to convey the complexity or the tangibility of the dream. Nonetheless, you've got to get it out, so you stumble through the surreal images and illogical episodes until you've managed to approximate some kind of verbal rendition of your dream.

No matter how bizarre the dream is, though, it's just a dream. No one judges you. You can't help the fact that Leonard DiCaprio is in love with you. You can't help the fact that a zombie is chasing you. We tend to find dreams entertaining and fascinating, rather than find the dreamer crazy or dishonest. We don't say, "Now wait a minute, you know quite well that there is no such thing as zombies, and that Leonardo DiCaprio only dates models with Daddy issues." We say, "Huh, how interesting." We even have dream experts that interpret dreams. It's kind of fun. But when you have a mental illness and you try to talk about what you are seeing and feeling, it's not really fun. You get frustrated because others can't feel or understand the same things you are feeling. Your friends and family are concerned because you have lost touch with reality. And, of course, you can't wake up to realize that what's happening is not real. Your dream is your reality.

Yet, I am here. I am ready to share my journey. I've tried my best here to describe what was going through my mind so you can get a better understanding of what it feels like to lose touch with reality. (That is, of course, if you haven't had the pleasure of experiencing this in your own life.) This special glimpse into this world might help you look at the mentally ill a little differently. What you see on the outside can't begin to explain what someone has been through on the inside. If this causes you to look at the mentally ill with compassion rather than judgement, then going on this journey was well worth it.

I am neither the genius of Vincent van Gogh, the thrusting lunatic of *Psycho* nor the incoherent homeless person. I may have been diagnosed with bipolar I disorder, but that is not who I am. It is something that I live with and treat. I am me. Educational program coordinator, stand-up comic, public speaker, athlete, sister, girlfriend, friend, writer, wannabe dancer and television expert, Maggie Newcomb. Although I was diagnosed with a pretty specific mental illness, I feel like my story is universal. We all are dealing with some sort of adversity, whether it be an illness, poverty, abuse, prejudice, whatever. We all want to find stability and balance in this crazy world we live in.

Another part of my decision to come out is due to an insatiable curiosity. I hope that the publication of my story will further a discussion of a topic that I find endlessly interesting: the human mind. I am intrigued by what happened to my own. The brain is so fascinating. What made me go crazy? What happened? Was there any truth in my enlightenment? Why was I able to come back to reality and others are not? Why is it taboo to talk about this? Most importantly, who will play me in the movie about my life?

In my thirty-seven years of life, I have experienced three major manic episodes associated with bipolar disorder. The first two occurred back-to-back in 1994, when I was sixteen years old. The third came in 2004, when I was twenty-six. Mania crept into my life and destroyed it for a time. Oh! But for a number of incredible days, what an experience it was! Here comes my crazy story, both the beautiful and the horrific. I will try my best to explain it. So sit back, buckle up, and enjoy the ride.

# the diagnosis

In order to understand how I got myself into God's Waiting Room and was about to cross over to heaven in 2004, we need to back up ten years to my first episodes.

It was 1994. I was a sophomore in high school, and I had just turned sixteen. I had shoulder-length blonde hair, silver braces, and a little bit of acne. The grunge look was all the rage, and all the cool kids had pagers. I tried to dress grunge, wearing baggy jeans and flannel shirts, but I just couldn't pull it off. I wasn't edgy or cool enough. I usually wore clothes from the clearance section at The Gap. I didn't have a pager either. This was partly because I couldn't afford it and partly because I was afraid if I got one that no one would page me.

I remember sitting in the lobby of the hospital with my parents and my psychiatrist. It was the last day of my ten-day hospitalization, and the doctor had requested a meeting with my parents and me to present the official *final* diagnosis. The lobby was quite nice, with cool, modern-style chairs and tables. There were floral arrangements on the tables and soft floral-print wallpaper. I sat there silently. My hair was pulled back into a ponytail, and I was wearing jeans and a hooded sweatshirt. My parents sat there nervously awaiting the final explanation for why their seemingly "normal" teenage daughter suddenly went crazy.

I was very interested in hearing the doctor's diagnosis. I knew I'd had some sort of emotional breakdown or even a "nervous breakdown," but I had no idea what either of those might mean. Nobody in the hospital had really told me anything about my condition during the ten days I had been there. They just gave me cups with pills in them. They made me take the pills in front of them, and then open my mouth to prove I had swallowed them. I had been through hours of individual and group counseling, forced to eat so I could take this mysterious medication, and even locked in a room by myself when I misbehaved.

I was physically and emotionally numb. I wanted to get out of there. I missed my dog and my bed. More than anything, I was very confused about what my life was going to be like in the days to come.

My doctor looked like Richard Dreyfuss from *Jaws*. In his classic brown suit, vest and tie, he gave out a 1980s busy, important-man vibe. Although the conversation was about my behavior, my disorder, and my future, he spoke to my parents as if I wasn't there. It was like I'd been found guilty of a crime and as I sat there in silence, he was the judge telling my parents the verdict.

He started with, "I want you to know that I am a Freudian psychiatrist." My dad seemed quite impressed with this credential. I wasn't exactly sure what that meant. My only reference to Sigmund Freud was from *Bill and Ted's Excellent Adventure*. I remember thinking, "What does that old man have to do with me? He doesn't know me."

Dr. Dreyfuss continued. "I have been treating your daughter for several days now. She has what is called bipolar I disorder otherwise known as manic depression. We came to this conclusion based on the fact that she experienced what is known as a manic episode. Also, her family history and response to the Lithium helped confirmed this diagnosis."

The three of us stared at him, struggling to comprehend. He continued. "She will have this illness for the rest of her life. She'll need to continue to take Lithium and other antidepressants." I could tell that my parents were scared. At one point he said, "We may want to consider keeping her back a grade. School may be too stressful for her." He tried to be more encouraging, telling us that I would feel better someday, but I started to tune him out like he was talking about someone else.

The diagnosis seemed so permanent and so strange. I had bipolar disorder? Manic depression? What? For some reason, when I thought of someone with manic depression I pictured a tortured artist at a spoken-word event, wearing all black and reading a poem about his depression after his favorite indie band that went triple platinum. That wasn't me. I couldn't even pull off the grunge look.

I didn't understand it at all. I couldn't process it.

To give you a better understanding of the diagnosis, the following is some background information about bipolar disorder from the National Institute of Mental Health and the National Association of Mental Illness. Most noticeably, the disorder can cause unusual shifts in mood, energy, and activity levels. Those with this disorder are vulnerable to very high "highs" called mania and very low "lows" called depression. There are two different types of bipolar disorder—I and II. Bipolar I disorder (the one I was diagnosed with) involves episodes of severe mood swings, from mania to depression, in which the acutely manic person usually needs immediate hospital care. However, he or she can have years of stability in between manic episodes. Bipolar II disorder is a milder form of the illness. It is characterized by what is called hypomania, which is a period of unusual and intense gaiety, confidence, excitement, irritation, or distraction. The elevated mood of hypomania can exist with or alternate with depression. Unlike someone diagnosed with bipolar I disorder, the person with bipolar II doesn't usually need to be hospitalized.

Mania is a state of mind that is commonly seen as the high point of bipolar disorder. NAMI lists manic symptoms such as feelings of excessive or disproportionate happiness that last for extended periods of time, overconfidence, increased talkativeness, racing thoughts, and decreased need for sleep. It is common for manic people to get delusional. Some claim that God is speaking to them directly or that they have godlike abilities. Although the manic person can be euphoric and excited, it's also very common for one to exhibit behavior that is not on the happy side and very negative. One may have increased irritability, agitated feelings, anger and be easily distracted. When some people become manic, they may be able to hide it and continue to exist in reality. When I experienced my third episode, I was able to do that for a while.

When mania is not treated it can often lead to psychosis, which is a fancy term for when someone's thoughts and emotions are so impaired that he or she has lost contact with external reality. People experiencing psychosis might envision themselves in a different place (okay, planet, maybe) than the one they're actually in. Or they might imagine that they're not themselves, or that someone they know has suddenly somehow transformed into something very different. Although someone who is in a state of psychosis is technically referred to as being psychotic, this is a bit annoying, because it can conjure up images of Jason or Freddie or any of a number of gross, knife-wielding or saw-waving movie maniacs. Someone who is psychotic is not necessarily someone who's violent; it's just someone who's not functioning in reality.

Someone can be both manic and psychotic at the same time. When this happens, it could be referred to as a severe manic episode with psychotic features, what I was hospitalized for. In the American Psychiatric Association's Diagnostic and Statistical Manual 5, a manic episode is characterized as "A distinct period of abnormally and persistently elevated, expansive, or irritable mood, lasting at least 1 week (or any duration if hospitalization is necessary)." It also states that "The mood disturbance is sufficiently severe to cause marked impairment in occupational functioning or in usual social activities or relationships with others, or to necessitate hospitalization to prevent harm to self or others, or there are psychotic features."

Sitting there with my parents listening to the doctor I knew my manic episode had ended, but it was just the beginning of my life with bipolar disorder.

As my parents and I left the hospital and headed for home, I started to feel incredibly guilty. This episode was all my fault. There was something wrong with me. I had brought on my breakdown. I must have not tried hard enough to be normal.

In the days to come, the shame and guilt started to eat away at me. I had no reason to be depressed or go crazy. I was never beaten or sexually abused. I didn't struggle in school. I didn't have to live in poverty. I had no good reason to develop this disorder! I had been given a beautiful life, and *I had ruined it*. I wished that I had cancer instead; at least with cancer you can prove it, and it's not your fault. I hated myself. I truly hated myself. I had caused all this pain. Maybe if I were more popular and had more friends, I wouldn't have gotten manic. These sorts of things didn't happen to the cool kids with pagers and excellent fashion sense.

For weeks after my hospitalization, I kept running through the events of the months before, searching for some sort of explanation. How could I have let this happen? How could I have done this to my family? Until a few weeks earlier, there had been no visible signs that I was a troubled teen.

In fact, up until age eleven, I was an absolute *superstar!*

# superstar

If I could hang out with anyone, I would hang out with my six-year-old self. Man, was she cool, like most six-year-olds can be. Maggie Newcomb—then Margaret Newcomb—was confident and in charge, full of attitude and sass, a burst of fresh air. Outgoing and very outspoken, this towhead with freckles knew that someday she was going to be a movie star. Margaret loved performing, and treated her family and friends to her original shows whenever the inspiration hit her. She often could be found dancing in the kitchen wearing a sailor dress while eating peanut butter and jelly sandwiches.

Her confidence seemed to override the fact that she wasn't necessarily the cutest or most coordinated little girl in her class. As school pictures can prove, Margaret was already the biggest kid in the class, even bigger than the boys. Not only didn't she fit into the clothes of her age group, but the clothes usually didn't match either. She refused to allow her mom to dress her. She was the driver of her own fashion mobile. She usually sported a mismatch of looks: striped pants with a plaid sweater or paisley skirts with polka-dots tights. Nailed it! She thought she looked great. No, she *knew* she looked great.

Margaret's dog Wilson was one of her closest companions. He was an old beagle mix that was extremely loveable and followed her everywhere she went. He smelled a bit—okay, maybe more than a bit—but he was adorable and Margaret loved him. She used to get the mean neighborhood kids to pet him and then tell them to smell their hands. She'd watch while they sniffed.

"Eeuuww, gross!" they'd whine. They'd get upset, and she would giggle.

At the age of ten, Margaret focused her dreams, deciding that instead of a movie star she was more suited for broadcast journalism. She knew she would be the next Diane Sawyer, constantly making videos with her friends for an adoring public, always the star. She even got a home perm and couldn't believe how good she looked. Weren't the 80s fun? She loved showing it off. There was no doubt in her mind that her future was bright. Whatever she wanted to be she knew she could make it happen.

Then puberty hit, and this confident star started to notice things. The other girls were smaller than her. In fact, when she compared herself to them, she looked like a giant. When she started to like boys, it became clear that none of them seemed to reciprocate. Her clothes somehow didn't fit right anymore, and this started to bother her, too. She looked in the mirror and saw a large, awkward body where she used to see a dancer. This was especially difficult to see. She became incredibly self-conscious and insecure. The superstar started to fade away.

As my star faded, my emotions and hormones started to get the best of me. Eventually I would start to have "secret" depressions. I tried to hide them from my family and friends. I didn't think to ask for help because I didn't realize what they were. I would tell my parents that I was taking a nap and then spend hours crying in my room. I thought that my extreme unhappiness was due to the fact that I wasn't liked enough, I didn't have enough friends or I wasn't popular enough. Gone was the brash, confident superstar of my younger days. All that I felt was unattractive and uncool.

Things got even tougher for me in high school. Not only did I start to dislike my appearance but I also started to dislike my personality. I felt that I was loud and obnoxious, and I'd tell myself to stop talking so much. I wanted desperately to be like the popular girls who always seemed to say the right things. And although throughout my life I usually had a nice group of friends, I never fully felt like I belonged anywhere. Yes, I had friends, but I wanted more. I felt like the Brazil nut or the banana runt of the group. I often felt very lonely. I was exhausted from the effort of trying to make others like me.

Although the childhood magic began to fall away, I remained active and involved. I was used to exerting a great deal of effort to succeed. I was an excellent student and got good grades. In high school I played sports like volleyball, basketball and track.

I tried to be social and go to the big parties, or "ragers" as we called them, whenever I could get myself invited. I experimented with alcohol and marijuana a couple of times, nothing major. I got drunk a couple of times at sleepovers. The usual: sneak into the parents' liquor cabinet and take a little out of each alcohol bottle so they didn't notice. Or get an older friend to buy us Zimas. I got high on marijuana a couple of times at a friend's house as well. I remember acting pretty stupid and saying very strange things, but luckily I was safe and nothing horrible came of it. I didn't seem to have any sort of addiction to alcohol or drugs. I thought they were fun, but I wasn't going to let them get in the way of my doing well in school. That may be thanks to a compelling episode of *Punky Brewster,* and to the D.A.R.E. campaign of the 1980s. From the outside I looked like an average teenager, trying to do well and trying to fit in.

Television became my escape. I loved sitcoms, in particular. Something about that studio audience with the laugh track made me feel safe. I was captivated by even the simplest story line. I wasn't allowed to watch TV during school nights, so on the weekends I got my fill. My earliest television memories are from watching *The Muppet Show*—man, how I loved the Muppets. Just hearing the theme song inspired me. Then I started watching primetime sitcoms like *The Facts of Life, Silver Spoons, 227,* and *The Golden Girls.* The good stuff. When I first started writing this book I wanted to name every chapter after a TV show. Like I'd have chapters named *"Gimme a Break!" "Family Ties,"* and *"Growing Pains."* Then I realized that not everyone is blessed with my obsession with television sitcoms.

As I got a little older in junior high I discovered stand-up comedy. The first stand-up show I watched was on VH1. It was called *Stand-up Spotlight* with Rosie O'Donnell. I was mesmerized by it. It made me laugh and think at the same time. It helped me escape into another world.

No matter how bad I was feeling, I could just turn on the TV, and for that one half-hour forget about my life and live vicariously through theirs. Television characters don't get depressed. Everything always works out in the end.

I needed some of that positive storytelling to help get me through high school. From the outside I probably seemed fine, but I was secretly struggling. Nobody could foresee what was about to happen to my family or me.

# the lead-up

My hospitalization took my whole family and community by surprise.

I grew up in what I am sure appeared to be a normal, happy suburban household. And in many ways it was. My family lived in a tract home from the 1970s, in a quiet residential suburb about thirty-five minutes from downtown San Diego. We had a nice backyard, and our remodeled house was bright and cheery, with hardwood floors and lots of plants.

I got along well with my parents and siblings, and our household was active and full of love. My mother, a beautiful, sensitive woman with dark, shiny hair and a heart of gold, was a graphic designer who gave up her career for almost two decades to raise us. My dad was a tall, blonde-haired, left-brained businessman who had a witty comment for every situation. My big brother, a student at the University of California, Santa Cruz during the time of my first hospitalization, was a tall, popular surfer. I looked up to him and wanted to be as cool as he was. My older sister was an attractive, brown-haired high school senior with a magnetic personality. Then there was me. In high school I was the little annoying sister who adored her siblings and would have done anything to be a part of their social lives. I loved my family. Sure we had our fights and our ups and downs like most families do, but I always felt supported and cared for.

With such a healthy home life it seemed unlikely that I would have a mental breakdown. However, there is always more going on than one can see from the outside. On my mother's side of the family there is a history of depression and alcoholism. However, it isn't something that was talked about. This information about my family history was important in determining my diagnosis. It could suggest that I was predisposed to mental illness.

My strange behavior started a couple of weeks prior to my hospitalization. It was March 1994, my sophomore year in high school. I was trying to do way too much and was extremely stressed out. I was playing three sports: club volleyball, swimming and track. I was also taking several honors classes. I was staying up late every night to complete a long, complicated research paper for a class project on Russian history. I began staying up later and later as I got more involved in the project. After working on it for hours, my mind was active and I was unable to sleep so I started sneaking Nyquil to help.

At first my parents thought I was depressed. I seemed to get upset very easily and would often cry in my room. This time I wasn't hiding it.

The tipping point came one weekend. That Friday was the talent show at my high school. I wanted to go, but I couldn't. I was stressed out, a little depressed, and plain old upset. I just didn't want to be around anyone. I spent the whole night by myself, thinking and thinking. I was trying to figure out why I was so unhappy. That weekend I moped around the house, alternating between watching television and hanging out in my room alone. I wasn't acting like myself. My parents, bewildered and concerned, decided that I should stay home from school the coming week since I was starting to act a little strange. They knew I was going through something, but they couldn't put their fingers on exactly what it was. They thought maybe I just needed a break from my hectic schedule.

To keep my mind off things and help me relax, my parents and I decided to rent some movies. We chose *Benny and Joon* starring Johnny Depp and Mary Stuart Masterson and *Dave* starring Kevin

Kline and Sigourney Weaver. I remember watching them and getting lost in the characters and storylines of each one. The themes were so fascinating! The movie *Dave*, in which Kevin Kline pretends to be the president of the United States, was speaking directly to me. I thought, aren't we all pretending to be something that we're not? Wasn't I pretending to be something else at school, making adjustments and reinventing myself in order to fit in and make friends? I got so lost in this message that, after a while, I wasn't really watching the movie anymore. I just sat there, thinking and thinking.

My mind started racing, one thought slamming into another, with another wave of thoughts and emotions close behind. My mind became a runaway train that was unstoppable and could crash at any minute. I couldn't stop thinking about the complexity of life. All the great universal themes flooded my mind: the nature of existence, our place in the universe, our relation to God.

The following days became a blur. I continued to have trouble sleeping and quieting my mind. At one point my mother said she found me in the fetal position on my bed, rattling on and on about one of my television shows. I was talking really fast and not making a lot of sense. That is when she knew something was seriously wrong. She called a friend who was a therapist to see what she should do. This friend recommended that she take me to get professional help and possibly even take me to the hospital. My mom called around and couldn't reach a doctor so she decided to wait until the next day to see how I was.

That evening I stayed up all night, just thinking. I still remember it to this day. I was sitting on my bed. It was dark. I was looking out the window of my bedroom and into the front yard. A gust of wind had risen, and the branches of our tree began to blow. I heard the rustling sound of the wind and saw the branches sway. Suddenly my whole being was filled with an overwhelming sense of peace. All these questions about life that I had been mulling around in my head for days, all the twisting, interconnected channels that led to longer and longer currents of thought finally came to a head.

I had it! All of a sudden I understood everything! It was God speaking to me. I didn't literally hear a voice, but nevertheless there was, in fact, one main message that I was receiving, and it was *a message sent directly from God to me:* I was special. Really special. I was stronger and more powerful than I had ever suspected. I had almost superhuman powers that others did not have. Between the feeling of strength and the feeling of knowledge, I knew that I had reached a radically new place in my life. I didn't know what to call it at the time. One might say that I had experienced enlightenment or a new heavenly existence, and at sixteen years old, that was pretty darn cool.

I had just discovered why I'd been so sad and unhappy for so many years. I was a genius, a prodigy! And neither the world nor I had suspected it. As I later wrote in my journal, "I felt like Charlie Gordon in *Flowers for Algernon,*" after he became super-intelligent.

Just like I would feel in God's Waiting Room ten years later, I had a knowing. An absolute knowingness of who I was and where I was headed. I was on a different level of understanding. I wanted so badly to share this with my family and the world. No one had to worry anymore. Everything was exactly as it should be. It was like heaven on earth.

That night I stayed up continuing to think about this new revelation. I never went to sleep. Then when morning came I raced into my parents' bedroom as they were getting ready for the day. I began to explain what had happened to me, all the thrilling revelations. I had so much to tell them. I was talking really fast, trying to keep up with my mind. My parents seemed to be trying, but could not understand what I was saying.

I was stunned. To me everything was so clear. To my parents, I was talking nonsense. I became confused and agitated at their reaction. My bizarre performance was extremely alarming. They had no idea what to do. They attempted to calm and understand me, but it was clear that I needed to get professional help.

My mom took me to my therapist, someone I had begun to see a few years earlier. I started to explain to her what I had learned the night before. I thought she was getting it. She was a professional, someone familiar with intellectual questions and realizations. She would get it, I knew she would. How great it would be when everyone understood the message that I had been given!

Later my therapist told me that I was talking so fast she couldn't understand me at all. I was completely incomprehensible. Right away she strongly suspected I was having a manic episode.

# first hospitalization

A t this point my family had no choice but to take me to the hospital. Luckily, there was a mental hospital very close by our house and close to my therapist's office. It was quite nice, nothing like the cold institutions you see in movies like *Girl, Interrupted.* But nonetheless, still a mental hospital. Since my dad had to go to work, my older sister stayed home from school to help my mom take me.

I didn't object to going to the hospital. A very small part of me was scared. However, a larger part of me thought it was just great! I figured that they wanted to study me, since I was a genius and probably had discovered the secret of the universe and all. Once I talked to them, they would understand it as well.

When I first got to the hospital my mom explained the situation to the staff. They told my mom that I was probably on drugs. My mom quickly said, "No, she's not on drugs."

"That's what all parents say," the nurse responded. However, after my blood test came back, they discovered that I was not on any drugs. Now this was both good and bad. Good that I didn't do drugs (again, thanks to *Punky Brewster* and a retired police officer from D.A.R.E.), but bad that there was no reason for me to act so crazy.

First, I was evaluated by a doctor. Shortly after I spoke with the doctor, he met with my mom and recommended that I be admitted immediately. In fact, according to the records the identifying data for my admission was stated as, "The patient is a single white female, admitted in an acute state of deterioration with depressed and psychotic features." My state was also described in records as "confusion, silliness, difficulty following directions, labile and inappropriate behavior, increased energy, flight of ideas." When my mother agreed to admit me, the nurse told her, "You don't know what a favor you're doing for your daughter. The majority of parents say 'no' and avoid treatment." My mother was filled with anguish signing the admission papers, wondering if she was doing the right thing.

After my mom and my sister left I was escorted to the section of the mental hospital where teenagers were treated. I was greeted by a woman who seemed like a nurse. She led me into a cold, barely lit room with a bed bolted to the floor, with straps attached to the sides and a very small window. I immediately froze, and a chill went down my back. It looked like one of those rooms that you saw in the movies. All that was missing was a person with a straightjacket. I turned around and looked at the nurse.

I think she could see the absolute shock and fear in my eyes. Then she said to me, "You aren't going to stay here. We just need to make sure you don't have anything that could hurt you. After I shut the door, take off all your clothes and put them into this bag. And I mean everything. Any jewelry, belts, shoes, everything. I'll take out anything that could harm you, and give you your clothes right back."

That made me feel a little better. I thought to myself, this is just a formality. They probably do this for the "other" patients that come here. I was sure the nurse and I both knew that I was neither sick nor dangerous. I took off all my clothes, put them into a bag, and put on the gown she'd handed me. I opened the door and gave my belongings to the nurse. She took the belt out of my pants, removed the shoelaces from my tennis shoes, and gave the bag back to me. Then I put my clothes back on, sans belt or shoelaces. That took a bit of getting used to.

After that, I sat down with the nurse and she asked me several questions. It was sort of like an intake form: How many hours did I sleep? What happened in school? When did these racing thoughts start? Her tone was very businesslike, with no emotion: no curiosity or sympathy. It was like talking to a DMV worker. I found her behavior strange. Why wasn't she more excited to talk about what was happening to me? The questions she asked seemed irrelevant in light of the amazing journey I was on.

After that, I went to my room to go to bed. They had given me a pill that was supposed to help me sleep. In the morning, I would meet with my doctor. My room was very basic, like a budget hotel room. A bed, dresser and small bathroom. I remember looking out the window and staring at the yellow pool of light that surrounded a lone light post in the empty parking lot. It seemed so peaceful. But a small part of me was scared. What was I doing here? I was sure that the next morning things would get better.

When the next day dawned, I looked around the room. I was frightened when I realized I wasn't home. I got in the fetal position and did something that for some reason made me feel better. Holding my legs I started yelling. "My name is Margaret Newcomb! I live on 5020 Hieldsberg Lane! My name is Margaret Newcomb and I live on 5020 Hieldsberg Lane! My name is Margaret Newcomb ..." I kept on yelling and yelling this until my new doctor walked in. "That is enough!" he yelled. "Stop that right now!" He clapped a few times trying to get me under control. I stopped and looked at him. It probably wasn't the greatest impression to make. I remember my doctor being very stern. Not mean, but not warm and fuzzy. He was very formal, wearing a crisp three-piece gray suit. As I mentioned he reminded me of Richard Dreyfuss, the early years. I didn't know it at the time but, despite his less than ideal bedside manner, he would be the one that would help lead me back to the real world, eventually.

He started me on Stelazine, an antipsychotic, and then eventually added Lithium. For some reason it didn't bother me that they made me take medication—at first. They gave me a little cup with several pills and told me to swallow them. In my mind these pills were inconsequential. They weren't going to impede my progress.

I was not aware of this, but the doctors told my family initially that I might have schizophrenia. However, they wanted to see how I responded to the medication before they made the final diagnosis.

The first day I tried to make the best of the situation. I journaled, and I sketched pictures of my surroundings. I thought these drawings were masterpieces, and was sure others would be impressed.

But then the medication quickly kicked in. I felt very strange, all hazy, drugged, and everything started to get fuzzy. Eventually, I could barely write in my journal. The drugs affected my ability to concentrate and even hold the pen firmly.

In the next couple of days, I started to question the whole situation. I didn't understand why I was still there. They were treating me just like they treated everyone else who was there, and the teenagers who were there seemed pretty weird. Some even scared me. I started to get more agitated. There must have been some sort of a mistake. Maybe I was too smart for them? Maybe they were trying to stop my journey? When they took my blood I wondered if maybe they were giving me a poison injection!

I didn't trust the staff. I'd had enough.

I felt that it was time for me to go home. They made no move to accommodate my wishes, and I got upset. I demanded to see my doctor. Although the medication made me feel drugged, I could still get angry. I remember yelling at the staff, explaining that I didn't belong there. I demanded again to see my doctor.

Finally the staff members gave in and said that I could see my doctor. The nurse and two of the counselors ushered me into a room. They told me that my doctor was in this room. I walked into the room, with the staff members all very close to me. I immediately recognized the room and knew that my doctor wasn't in there.

They had led me into the room where they'd made me take my clothes off when I first arrived. They called it the "seclusion room," which is a nice way of saying "solitary confinement." Wait! Why was I in here? I tried to step back to get out, but they were holding on to me. In one move they lifted me onto the bed. They held my arms back and my legs down. I remember one of the counselors looking at me and saying, "I'm sorry."

Then they brought out a syringe, pulled my shorts up on one leg, and injected something into my thigh. Despite my resisting them, they managed to tie down my arms and legs with the straps attached to the bolted bed. The medication immediately kicked in and I calmed down. Then they all left the room.

I was there, alone. I remember hearing a beep, like something you hear in a hospital room, but I think that was just my imagination. The seclusion room quickly faded. The next day I woke up in my own room. They must have moved me in my sleep.

Unfortunately, that would not be my only visit to the seclusion room. As I was still manic, my memory is not clear, but the next day or so, as a group of us were watching an inspirational video, I guess I got disruptive. All I remember is that somehow I was on the floor, and I was crawling around. I have no idea why I did this. The staff was, once again, all around me.

They put me back in the cold, barely lit room with the bed bolted to the floor. They didn't need to restrain me anymore. After the first time I went willingly. They'd put a tray of food inside the room for me to eat. I would have to eat most of it and take these pills (which I later learned were Lithium) before they'd let me out. It felt like I had been bad, and was being punished. If I wasn't let out I would usually just fall asleep in the room. One time I remember waking up in the seclusion room, and my mom was sitting next to me. She was crying. They normally didn't allow family members in that room, but this time they made an exception.

After those first several days in the hospital passed, it didn't seem like I was making much progress. I wasn't following direction unless I was forced. Therefore, they brought in my sister and my mom to encourage me to go along with the program. I actually don't remember this part. My sister told me that I wouldn't let anyone touch me. And I had started refusing to take the medications. I acted like it was me against the staff. I had been in the seclusion room so much that I explained to my sister I developed tricks to outsmart the staff. I would pretend to faint so they would have to come get me. I don't remember that at all, but I am sort of proud of my crafty manic strategy.

I am not sure how my sister and mom did it, but they convinced me to trust the staff and do what they asked. I think they would have done anything to help me come back. It was very hard for them to see me this way. I was still not the sister and daughter they knew. They visited me as much as possible. My sister even had to help me take a shower and brush my hair. I was in the throes of mania and it was thanks to my mom and my sister who continued to visit me and support me that helped me take advantage of the treatment.

I had many group and individual therapies. My doctor was all business in our meetings. He reminded me of a detective trying to solve the mystery: the mystery of my diagnosis. He found out the details of my family history and questioned me on all the events that led to my downfall. He was very dedicated to solving this puzzle. He seemed very knowledgeable and I trusted him. In some ways I was glad that he was leading the investigation and treatment. It might have been nice to have a doctor that was a little more nurturing, but at least I had someone very capable on my team.

After several days on the medications, I eventually came out of the mania. It is hard to explain how that happens. It's sort of like waking up from a dream. I slowly started to realize where I was, and why I had been brought there. I was not special. Nor did I have any magic powers. All those things I'd realized about the secrets of the universe: I couldn't remember them anymore. Everything that was once so clear became shrouded with haziness and fog. I didn't understand anything. The brilliant images and breathtaking realizations, that genius knowledge had slowly, somehow slipped through my fingers. It was as if all of it had been the delusions of a child.

I started acting normal again. No fast talking, no outrageous ideas. I did everything the staff asked me to do. Toward the end of the hospitalization, I felt terrible about my actions. As the doctor wrote in my records I often said that I had "let everyone down." After being in the hospital for ten days, I was ready to be released. On that last day at the hospital I got that final diagnosis from the doctor of bipolar I disorder. It confirmed that I wasn't enlightened. I was just ... crazy.

# recovery and relapse

I went right back to school shortly after I got out of the hospital. People were very nice to me upon my return, but it was awkward for me. Some of my friends had made me a "welcome back" card. Despite the support, I wasn't sure what to tell people about where I had been. I was never entirely sure how to talk with them when I was feeling "normal," and now that I had just been in a mental hospital, I was even more confused.

I was fortunate to go to a very good school, but it was one that I never quite felt comfortable in. It was in a nice area, an area that my family didn't live in. My siblings and I received an inter-district transfer, which allowed us to attend a really great high school, instead of the one near our house. It was a beautiful campus with perfect landscaping and large oak, palm, and fern pine trees. Even in my sophomore year, I was still intimidated by all the rich kids in their BMWs and Jeep Grand Cherokees.

My family and I decided that I should be honest. If anyone asked where I was I would say something like, "I have bipolar I disorder, and I had a manic episode that put me in the hospital for a while." I rehearsed it until I had it down. The first time people asked where I had been, I told them. Their eyes widened. They were like, "Uh … wow. …" It was so awkward. I could tell they wanted to support me but were very uncomfortable. They had absolutely no idea what to say to me. I mean, most adults don't even know what a manic episode really is. How could I expect high school kids to do better?

I still had so many questions! Now that I was out of the hospital, was I cured? Was I going to be okay? Nobody knew. There weren't any bipolar role models for me to look up to. It was uncharted territory for everyone. I still felt overwhelming shame and embarrassment about the whole thing.

Reentering the world I had known did not go very well. I dove back in to my schedule just like everything was fine and dandy, but it wasn't. First, I was still adjusting to the side effects of all the medications. My mom was in charge of the medications. She would make sure that I took them morning and night. She made little pill cases for me. I didn't protest. I would do anything not to go back to the hospital. As I got used to the medications, that druggy spaceyness slowly went away. The nausea was still there. I believe it was from the Lithium. It was brutal.

I threw up so much from the Lithium that I actually got used to throwing up. Remember when you were a kid, and you were so afraid to vomit? After a while, it was like, no big deal. It still felt awful, but it wasn't scary anymore. In the hospital we weren't allowed to flush the toilet after throwing up. We had to show our hurled masterpiece to one of the staff. I'm not sure, but I think they were checking to see if our pills were in the vomit.

I remember that the vomiting continued even after I got home from that first hospitalization. I threw up more in the days following the hospital than any model during fashion week. I puked in my room on the carpet, and my dad had to help me clean it up. I was so embarrassed. One time I was talking on the phone in the kitchen, and then all of a sudden I puked in the sink. On the way to school, my mom had to pull over so I could deposit some puke on the roadside. I sprinted out of math class one day and got to the bathroom just in time to ... you know ... puke.

The medication also affected my concentration and my balance. I wasn't as good at volleyball anymore, and my club volleyball coach demoted me to a lower team. Lithium also made me gain a little weight. I was a little bit thicker. It might be because I could only take Lithium on a full stomach. If I tried to take it without enough food in my stomach I would get horribly ill, with stomach pains and nausea. It was awful. Every time I ate a meal, I needed to take my meds. It was like I was a Pavlovian dog. After any meal I was like, where are my meds? I felt incomplete if I ate and didn't take something.

Despite the side effects, I continued to take the medication. Unfortunately, my painstaking efforts were not enough. My academics slipped, and I struggled to keep up in my honors classes. A little over a month after that first episode, I relapsed. I had tried to go back to school too soon. The stress of trying to fit in with my friends, catch up with my schoolwork, and keep up with my extracurricular activities overwhelmed me.

This second episode is very hard for me to talk about. This time, the mania came on a lot quicker and was much stronger. The intense emotions that engulfed me were less fun, and were less enlightening. This time, I didn't have any visions from God.

It started on a Friday night, after I'd gone to the movies with a friend. The film that we saw was the comedy-drama *With Honors.* The main character, played by Brendan Fraser, is obsessed with graduating from Harvard with honors, but a homeless person, played by Joe Pesci, thwarts his efforts and teaches him that there's more to life than ambition.

The more I pondered the theme of the movie, the more it intrigued me. The complexity of the message was so interesting. The central character's tunnel-vision approach to success made me think about my own life, and how I had always worked so hard to be the best. The movie was over, but I couldn't stop thinking about it. The pace of my thoughts accelerated, picking up speed until they started to take over my brain. The world around me didn't matter anymore. I felt lost in my mind. I couldn't stop thinking about it and other life issues. Before long, the train had left the station. By Monday I wasn't making sense. My thoughts were uncontrollable, and the onslaught of thoughts cascaded into mania. Who knew a Brendan Fraser movie would drive me over the edge?

As the mania took over, I did some pretty strange things. I wrote really weird things in my journal. I drew pages of swiggly lines. I wrote a big *L* on one page, then an *I* on the next until it spelled out Lithium. I did weird things, too, like pour 7UP on a plant because I thought I was watering it. Food tasted different. I was eating pancakes, but they tasted like onions and garlic. I was almost totally gone. Lost again in my mind. My parents had to take me to the hospital.

I arrived at the hospital, and I couldn't stop crying. Records show that I was "admitted in a state of decompensation and confusion." They put me in the seclusion room. I didn't protest, so they didn't need to restrain me. I thought I was in there for maybe a day, but later another patient told me I was in there for two days. The mania had turned into severe psychosis. I wasn't violent; I just wasn't there. I was in a different world, and it was terrifying. I slept on that bed bolted to the floor, drifting in and out of consciousness. Time had no meaning at all. It was very confusing, and I didn't understand where my mind was taking me. This time I was not in a dream, as I had been for most of the first episode. This time I was in a nightmare, and I could not wake up.

Have you ever been really sick with a fever, and had weird dreams? Fever dreams? My time in the seclusion room was one long chain of such dreams, an endless hallucination filled with bizarre symbols and haunting locations that meant nothing to me. That is what remains with me the most from this episode: being in the seclusion room. My body was there, but my mind had checked out. It had traveled to and gotten lost in the harrowing delusions of its own creation. At one point, I remember waking up in the middle of the night. I opened my eyes and saw three people looking down at me. They were talking about me, but I couldn't understand them. They were standing right next to me, but they felt worlds away. I drifted back to sleep.

When I finally awoke from these strange delusions and became fully conscious of where I was, I remember getting out of bed and going into the bathroom attached to the seclusion room. I looked in the mirror and was shocked at what I saw. My face was pale and my eyes looked empty. My hair was so messy that it almost looked like I had blond dreadlocks. I didn't recognize myself. I looked like Kurt Cobain. It was very difficult to see myself in that state. It wasn't cool. I wasn't a rock star, I just looked like a mental patient.

The staff tried different medication combinations on me, and found one that seemed to work. I slowly came out of the episode. I know that they finally settled on a combination of Lithium, Wellbutrin and Depakote. After more than a week of intense treatment, I was no longer in a manic psychosis. I was acting normal again. However, I was numb. This time I almost didn't want to come home, because this time I knew how hard it would be to fight my way back. I didn't want to have to explain what had happened, again. I didn't even understand it.

Once more, I was overcome with guilt and shame. Words can't express how awful I felt about myself. I had caused a repeat of this horrible experience. It was my fault. I struggled with depression for months after I was released. I was acting normal but a hazy cloud of depression lingered about me. I felt terrible about myself. I felt worthless. I hated myself. Luckily, I had access to aggressive professional treatment. I saw my psychiatrist and therapist regularly to help me get through the depression. I kept going and focused on the future.

Over the course of the next several months, my hair started falling out. Oh, my beautiful hair! They weren't sure if it was due to the Depakote or to the stress of the episode, but away it went. This was so sad for a sixteen-year-old girl with self-esteem issues! I am not sure exactly how much fell out. I wore it in pony tail, hoping people wouldn't notice how tiny the ponytail actually was. If I had to guess I would maybe say about one-third fell out. Then it started growing back—curlier. I had to finally cut it real short, like almost boy-haircut short. It looked awful. Unlike the cool third-grader with the home perm, the teenage Maggie could not pull off short, curly hair. Not only were no guys interested in me with long hair, with this haircut now there was no hope. Whether it was the hair or not, there would be no boys for Maggie until many years later.

As I dealt with the medication over the course of the next several months, the side effects slowly went away. I became accustomed to taking this trio of pills and did so for a while.

I didn't finish the school year, so I had to go to summer school and attend a program for troubled teens. It was a school that barely felt like a school. Most of the classrooms were in portable buildings. These kids intimidated me even more than the kids from my own high school. These were the kids who got kicked out of school or for some reason couldn't finish. Since it was the 90s, these were the bad-ass grunge kids with the baggy pants and skater t-shirts who smoked after school. And they all seemed to know each other. I don't think I said one word at this school. I just watched them, and prayed they didn't make fun of me. I did my math, science and English work as fast as I could and counted the days until it was over.

In the fall I came back to school full-time for my junior year. I tried to act like the episode had never happened. I think everyone else did too. Again, people wanted to support me, but they just didn't know how. Nobody ever talked about either the episode or my illness, no one asked about it or ever brought it up. It was that which would not be spoken of. It was my Voldemort.

Although I struggled at school, my family was there for me. They all supported me the best way they could. I could tell that my dad didn't fully understand the disorder and in some ways was afraid of it, but he tried never to show it. My mom was extremely diligent about my treatment. She made sure I went to my psychiatric appointments and that I took my medications. She did everything that she could to help me stay healthy. She bought all kind of books to learn more about it. She even took me to see an acupuncturist. She told me, many times, to never give up.

My sister was sort of my protector. She helped take care of me when I was manic and was there to support me with the recovery. She dealt with all the rumors swirling around school, rumors about me and about where I had been. Although she didn't fully understand what happened, she did her best to stick up for me. My brother used humor to deal with the situation. He told me that I should just own the whole "crazy" thing. He suggested I wear all black, put cat hair all over me and sit in the back of the classroom staring off into space. Just to see the reaction of the class. I think he had recently seen the movie *The Breakfast Club,* and he wanted me to be that weird character played by Ally Sheedy. We both had a good laugh at the concept.

I did the best I could to go back to my old life and keep going. However, it was harder than I had anticipated. This time I wasn't just demoted from the volleyball team, I was cut completely when I tried out for varsity my junior year. It was the only sport I was still playing. I was sad that I was no longer part of a team and missed that feeling of belonging somewhere. I thought maybe I would try something different. I thought maybe I should try to be in the drama club and hang out with other misunderstood folks. I tried out for a play, but didn't get cast in any of the roles. Not even a walk-on. I then tried out for the improv team. They did improvisational comedy competitions with other schools. I didn't make the team, but I did make the second string, the B team. So if someone on the team got hurt while pretending to do something, I would be there.

I was pretty miserable throughout the remainder of high school. From the outside I appeared to be doing well. I was getting good grades and hanging out with friends. The insecurities I'd felt before were still there, but now they were amplified by the fact that I had something to hide. I wanted, desperately, to be someone else, someone who could be comfortable, someone who could fit in with the cool kids. Looking back, I see someone whose goals were pretty shallow. I'm sure that in my attempts to be popular, I overlooked some really cool people. I regret that. Now I wish that I'd expanded my view. But at that wrenching time, all of my energy was directed to trying to survive my own life. I had no idea how to feel at home, to feel at ease in my own skin. I believed that being popular was the only way that I could do this.

Toward the end of high school, after one of my routine blood tests to check my Lithium levels, they discovered that I had a thyroid disorder. I had been feeling tired for months, but I just thought I was not getting enough sleep. The disorder was not a surprise to my doctor. Lithium can often damage the thyroid. I had to take medication to correct it. I think if that were to have happened later in my life, I would have been upset about it. At that young age I was just like, whatever. I didn't really think about it too much. It was just another pill for me to take.

With the medication and psychotherapy treatment, I stayed in school and was finally able to graduate. Many people ask me how I got through it. To be honest, I didn't really have a master plan. Things *slowly* got better. I started to forget about the episodes. I think it helped that I was a teenager. My mom was able to make sure that I took my medication. I think it also helped that there was no Internet at the time. Had I seen the statistics for relapse and failure for those with bipolar disorder, I would have wanted to give up. I didn't know any different. I didn't think I had any other choice than to just move on. I didn't accept it or feel good about it. I just kept going.

I think it also helped that my episodes were so scary and so agonizing that I would have done anything to prevent another one. The confusion of mania and the depression that followed were just the beginning of pain. The struggle to reenter a world that doesn't welcome difference, especially not mental illness, was the continuation.

I never wanted to go through that again, not for as long as I lived. I vowed to do whatever it took to stay stable and avoid the hospital.

Therefore I continued to take meds and see my doctor regularly. In some ways he was very encouraging, constantly reminding me that I could treat the illness and live a good life. He made sure to explain that the key to my recovery was staying on the medications. I learned that many people had relapses when they went off their medications. If staying out of the mental hospital meant taking stupid pills for the rest of my life, I would do it.

More than anything I think the thing that helped the most was that no matter how miserable I was, something deep inside told me that my misery was only temporary. I knew that if I could just get through high school, there was a chance that I could go away to college. Then I could really start over.

I didn't want anything to do with enlightenment. I just wanted to feel normal, and maybe someday even have a boyfriend.

# 10 years of stability

On the drive to college I could hardly contain my excitement. It was the end of the summer of 1996. I had worked hard to get accepted to the University of California, Davis, a large campus tucked into an idyllic college town in the northern part of the state. Thanks to a small government grant, a lot of student loans, and help from my parents, I was on my way.

My mom and my dad drove with me from San Diego to Davis to help me move into the dorms. Usually it's about an eight-to-nine-hour drive, but with my bike strapped to the top of our station wagon and my dad driving, it took about eleven hours. Not that I minded. I spent most of the drive listening to my new audiotape of Tony Robbins's *Awaken the Giant Within.* I stared out the window at the miles of tomato, almond, apricot, and asparagus fields that we drove past. California's Central Valley with Tony Robbins's voice in my ear, telling me how great life could be.

I was so ready to start over! And Tony was just the person to help make it happen. Since my episodes, I had become obsessed with self-help books. Their positive words helped get me through the shame and depression that followed my hospitalizations.

It turned out that with my entry into college at Davis, I actually *was* able to start over. My determination to stay on my meds and my positive mindset enabled me to create a new life. I wasn't

Margaret—that girl that was in the mental hospital who may or may not be crazy. I was Maggie—a college student, with a future as bright as the future of any new student on campus.

In order to move forward, I made the decision that I would not talk about my illness with others. People didn't need to know about it. That's when I developed my "don't ask, don't tell" policy. Fortunately, asking someone if they have bipolar disorder is not really a question that anyone usually asks. So it never came up. Despite the fact that I secretly took pills morning and night, I was no longer that crazy girl in high school. No one knew that I was anything but normal.

One of the perks of going to a university was that I was under the care of a university psychiatrist for free. Unfortunately, the one assigned to me wasn't anything special. He was another middle-aged white guy with a beard and a high opinion—of his own opinion. He mostly just prescribed me my medication and listened to a few of my stories. Although he wasn't great, I still received professional treatment, and in this way was able to remain stable and avoid major episodes. I stayed on my medications. I also made sure not to take on too much, so that I didn't get overwhelmed. I made it a rule to not exceed twelve units per quarter the first year, and I limited the number of challenging classes I took each semester.

My dad encouraged me to follow in the tradition of his mother and join a sorority. I wasn't sure that I was the sorority type, but I liked the idea of belonging to a group of friends. I went through the first day of "rush," where you walk to each house and talk to the different girls. The experience felt very strange to me. The girls were nice but reminded me of talking robots from a sci-fi movie. Fembots. They were almost too nice. And the matching outfits and singing were more than I could take. I dropped out after the first day.

Luckily, I really liked my suitemates in the dorm. I started to become close friends with two of them. The three of us began to eat meals together, stay up late talking, and go to parties. Eventually it became harder and harder to hide my medications from them. At that time I was on Lithium and Wellbutrin. I had tapered off the Depakote.

One night we stayed up late talking and I told them about my episodes and my diagnosis. I was prepared for them to feel uncomfortable and pull away. They both surprised me. They were completely supportive and accepting. In fact, the aunt of one of my new friends had been diagnosed with a mental illness as well. She understood a little of what I had been through. Although I was happy that they accepted me, I decided that, for the most part, I would continue to keep my illness a secret from everyone else.

The three of us were quite the social butterflies. We had to go to all the cool parties, sneaking into them most of the time. I had made the decision that it would be okay if I drank alcohol while on my medications. My psychiatrist mentioned that when I was twenty-one I would be able to have a drink or two. So it wasn't like I was completely disobeying doctor's orders. It was sort of my version of stretching the truth. At the age of eighteen, I felt that I was mature and was emotionally ready to start drinking. And if it was more than a drink or two, I was sure that it would be okay.

I was very, very lucky. Drinking didn't seem to affect me, or my medications, in a negative way. It didn't cause an episode. I enjoyed drinking, but I was responsible. My friends and I looked out for each other, too. We didn't let the weekend parties interfere with our schoolwork. I drank to socialize—not to cope or to numb. Well, on second thought, I may have used alcohol to help me feel more comfortable talking with guys. At parties I used to pretend to spill my drink on a cute guy to start a conversation. It actually worked a couple of times. Quite genius, if you ask me.

Although I was okay, I wouldn't advocate drinking for anyone on medication. I know that alcohol can often negatively affect those with a mental illness and their use of medication. In fact it can be very dangerous. Again, I may have just been lucky.

Not only did I enjoy the social life in college, I loved the academics. I believe one reason I was able to achieve stability at this point in my life was that I pursued things that I was passionate about. I chose to study international relations, business, and Spanish. I had dreams of being a successful businesswoman or diplomat. I wanted to be the CEO of a company, or maybe even get into politics. I was drawn to international relations, in part because I always dreamed of living abroad. When I was in grade school I wanted to be a foreign exchange student. Something about being in another country— visiting places I'd only read about or never even heard of—just excited me. I also loved learning about other cultures. When I was in high school my diagnosis of mental illness and the pain that surrounded it made me long to escape my own life. The desire to know other countries grew.

I chose Spanish because I fell in love with the language. It was so beautiful, and I noticed that whenever I spoke Spanish, I just plain felt *good*. I discovered recently that the part of our brain that processes language is far away from the part that produces anxiety. Maybe speaking Spanish strengthened my good-brain muscle, which helped me avoid mental breakdowns. I don't know exactly how it happened, and I apologize to experts for my unsophisticated analysis. All I know is that it helped me feel better.

After my sophomore year I realized one of my childhood dreams: I spent a summer studying in Spain. I had to beg my insurance company to pay for two months of medication. In the late 1990s, insurance companies would only allow for one month of medication at a time, but I managed to convince them. With what I had been through with my mental illness, my parents, of course, were worried about me traveling, but they let me go. They knew how important it was to me.

Spain was wonderful, and I had an incredible time! Each day began with a lesson in Spanish on the country's history or culture. I got to learn all these fascinating things about this beautiful country, and afterwards I was able to travel through it. I loved the culture and the lifestyle. Just like at Davis, I was responsible, but still had fun. I was twenty at the time, and legally allowed to drink alcohol in Spain. So I did. I continued to take my meds and have a few drinks at night. I didn't do anything crazy. I may have danced with a few Spaniards, but nothing outrageous. *Me gustaba bailar con los hombres de Espana! Ole!* ("I loved to dance with Spanish men.")

In college, I also had the opportunity to try out for the UC Davis Women's Rowing team. My suitemate rowed crew our freshman year and convinced me to go out for the team in my sophomore year. Even with my average athletic ability, I made the team. My height was a major factor: taller people have a longer stroke in the boat, and this can make them row faster. I was put in the novice team with other novice rowers, and together we slowly learned how to row. Learning to row was one of the hardest and most rewarding things I have ever done. As anyone who has ever committed to it can tell you, it takes skill, patience and strength.

Just like I felt when speaking Spanish, when I was rowing on the water I did not feel depressed. Any problems I had disappeared when I was on the water. I actually felt good about myself. So I stuck with it, no matter how mentally and physically challenging it was. I rowed on the UC Davis crew team for four years (I was on the five-year college plan). And I loved it. The water was so beautiful. We would get to the Boathouse in the Port of Sacramento when it was still dark and row while the sun came up. The water glistened as the blades of our oars sliced into it. Working out every day really helped my mental health in general, and following a strict schedule was very good for my bipolar condition. I focused on the sport rather than on drinking, parties, worry or stress. And the team became my family. Being around a bunch of strong, supportive women helped me with my self-esteem. We were all awkward, big girls, most of whom desperately wanted a boyfriend. Whatever our quirks or idiosyncrasies, however, we accepted each other unequivocally. More important, every day the men's team, in their tight spandex, walked the boats down from the boathouse. And we got to watch.

Unfortunately, I struggled with the competition part of it. I was afraid I would mess up and let everybody down. Before every race I was filled with overpowering anxiety and fear. What if I wasn't good enough? What if I caused our top boat to lose? What if I caught a crab? ("Catching a crab" means rowing too deeply, which can get the oar stuck and cause a lot of problems. Probably not what you thought it might mean.) I began to dread races. In the days before our competitions, I would have nightmares about my performance. I prayed that the race would be canceled.

I decided I needed to confront this dilemma. So I brought my old friend Tony Robbins back into my life. I listened to his words of encouragement. I did positive visualizations before each race. I tried meditating as well. I would listen to other motivational speakers, like Wayne Dyer. With his help I was able, for the most part, to manage my fears, but I never really acquired the competitive edge that some of my teammates did. I kept my anxieties to myself and just tried to be part of the team.

Like many students, I had to work during college to make ends meet. I got a job at the Coffee House on campus as a food-service worker and dishwasher. After a year I worked my way up to supervisor, which meant I got to wear a red apron. It doesn't sound like a big deal, oh but it *was*.

Finally, for the first time in my life, I felt like I had everything under control. My academics were good, I had a job, I was in the top boat, and—wait for it—I was in my first relationship. With a guy, a real guy. Everything that I had worked so hard for had come to fruition. Life was perfect. I began to think, do I really need to be on all of my medications? I was still on two psych meds, Lithium for mania and Wellbutrin for depression.

I wasn't thinking about going off *all* of them; I wouldn't do anything stupid without my doctor's approval. What if I just went off one, I thought? I wouldn't technically be going off my meds. But on one medication, I thought, I would be one step closer to being normal.

The idea of being normal was—is—exhilarating. No matter how many years I have accepted the fact that I need medication, the idea of going off of it brings up strong emotions. In some ways I imagine that it could be like being adopted, and longing to know your real parents. You love your life with your adopted parents (your life on meds). You're doing well, you're being good, but deep down you have this strong desire to know your real parents (your real self, you off medications). Maybe it was a mistake and your real parents didn't want to give you up (maybe you don't have a mental illness). Just the thought of knowing that your real parents didn't abandon you, that they're still out there somewhere, wanting to meet you, is intensely amazing. If I did not take meds I could maybe meet the person I really, truly was, and maybe this real me wouldn't have an illness. Just the thought of it was tempting. There will always be a part of me that longs, that aches, that dreams to be without medication, no matter how much I know I need it.

I convinced my doctor that I was in a good place and I should try to go off one of my medications. We decided that I could start tapering off Wellbutrin, the antidepressant. I would still be on Lithium, which helps with the mania. I felt like I was ready. It sounded like a good plan. Boy, was I wrong.

A month after I went off Wellbutrin, things began to go downhill. My rowing was affected, and I had trouble managing the mounting anxiety. I started to lose my confidence as a rower on the team. Eventually I lost my seat in the top boat. I got demoted from the varsity to the junior varsity boat, and then to the third boat. Perhaps this was not a huge event in one's college career, but to me, it felt like the world was crashing down around me. Looking back, it doesn't seem like a huge deal. However, at the time I was devastated. I felt like my life had completely fallen apart. I didn't think I would ever get over it. I was so angry with myself. How could I have let this happen?

After the demotions, life did not seem worth living. I was so ashamed of my performance that I became suicidal. Like the covert operative that I am, I kept my state of mind a secret from my friends. They knew I was upset, but I never told them how upset. In my vulnerable state, I didn't know how to cope. I became paralyzed with depression and fear and could not function. From my narrow perspective, I felt I had no reason to live. Part of me was able to get enough distance to realize that I had never felt this terrible before about something so minor. Fortunately, I was smart enough to talk to my doctor about it. We both decided I should go back on Wellbutrin.

Slowly, after a few weeks, my confidence came back. I was no longer suicidal. I could function again. I was so glad to come out of the depression that I didn't mind that I once again had two medications to take. I had to come to terms with the fact that I would have to take more than one medication, at least for a while.

Even on my medications, I would still struggle at times. Just like everyone, I had my ups and downs. Medication is not magic. I know that it helped keep me balanced and manage the extreme arc of my moods. I would still have to deal with major depressions after difficult life events. However, I was able to come out of them eventually. Breakups were always the hardest—mostly because I was usually the one getting dumped. Man, that would hurt. One of my college boyfriends broke up with me at a rest stop on our way down the 101 to Santa Barbara. Can you believe it? Somewhere near San Luis Obispo, I got my heart broken. I spent the rest of the drive sobbing. I tried to pretend like it was mutual, but I think my begging him to take me back gave that away. I still feel a pang of sadness every time I stop at a rest stop.

After I graduated from UC Davis, I wasn't sure exactly what type of job I would try to get, but I knew I wanted to live in another country. I went to the career center on campus and told them that I wanted to live abroad. They helped me find a four-month internship in Argentina at an English institute. So I took it.

Teaching English in Argentina was a lot of fun and a whole lot of hard work. I fell in love with the country. The insurance company put its foot down this time and refused to approve the four months of medication I would need to get me through my internship, so this time I got my meds in Argentina. After my one-month supply was gone, I took my bottles to one of the farmacias in the very small town I lived in. The pharmacist had to research what the meds translated to in Spanish. Then she had to order them from Germany. It was time-consuming, but doable. I had to hide my meds from my host family so they didn't think I was crazy, which I was. They already thought I was weird because I put peanut butter on my toast in the morning instead of *dulce de leche*. Dulce de leche is like caramel. Who eats caramel for breakfast?

Upon my return from Argentina I got a job at Oakley Inc. in Orange Country as an international something-or-other. (The job was so nondescript that the title is irrelevant.) I didn't like working in Orange County. No offense, Orange County, but to me, living there was like constantly stepping onto a *Star Trek* holodeck: all of the inhabitants were pretty much the same, and all of them were a little too tan, rich and perfect. I decided to move to Oakland to be with my two best friends from college. It was a risky move leaving a stable job, but I did it.

I packed up my stuff and moved to Oakland to live with my friends. After many months of applying for work, I finally landed a job at a law office as an administrative assistant. I also helped coach rowing for the Berkeley High School rowing team. I was in a pretty good place.

It had been about nine years since my episode at the age of sixteen. I had far surpassed my doctors' expectations; I had graduated not only from high school but from college. I had secured two professional jobs, either in or related to my major. And I had experienced *no more episodes.*

I just gave you the *Cliff's Notes* version of my life during these years for a reason. I want to get to the good parts. I want to get back to God's Waiting Room, where things get really exciting. If this were a movie I would show these past ten years as a montage with cool music underneath, like the *Rocky* theme. I would show clips of me rowing on the water in the early-morning light, raising my hand in class, working hard at my Coffee House job, crying in my room, reluctantly looking at my pills and then taking them, dancing the merengue in Spain, and finally tossing my hat in the air on graduation day at the end of college.

Despite some ups and major downs, I was finally in a stable place. The past several years were no walk in the park and it had taken a lot of work to get to this point. There were many low points that I wasn't sure that I would get through. However, I had kept moving forward, one adventure to the next. First was high school, then college, and then the working world. I focused on what I wanted to do and not on what I couldn't do. More important, taking care of myself and continuing treatment was my first priority. The memory of my hospitalization began to fade. Eventually, my family started to forget that I had ever had an illness. I was truly living a normal life.

And my new life in Oakland would bring exciting new opportunities that would change my life forever.

# bipolar comedian?

It was the summer of 2003. I had been living in Oakland, California for a little under a year, with four other people in a big, beautiful Victorian home near Lake Merritt. Two of my roommates were close friends that I had already lived with in college at Davis, and the other two were new friends we had met. Since there were so many of us, we were able to afford to live in a picturesque two-story home, full of history and character, in a neighborhood that was a mix of funky-cool and nice residential. The house was built in 1908 but was still in great condition. The hardwood floors and classic wood paneling were a deep, rich brown that shone. It was such a cool place to live with friends.

I was working full time and getting ready to start coaching crew for the fall. I was doing okay. Not bad, but not great. I was stable, but still recovering from a breakup a few months earlier. Okay, it was like a year earlier, but it still hurt. One day my sister called me. It was a typically lovely Northern California day in late July, sunny and clear.

"Maggs, I just found something I think you should try."

"Really? What?" I replied. She went on.

"There's a coffee shop in Berkeley that has an open mic night on Tuesday. Anyone can sign up and perform stand-up."

I was silent. The idea excited and frightened me. I had been obsessed with stand-up comedy since junior high. My sister's suggestion brought up vivid memories of all those lonely Friday and Saturday nights when I was growing up. I watched it on television and loved every moment of it. I would pretend to do sets in front of my stuffed animals. I would put them all in a line and stand in front of them with the broom. *To be read with a Jerry Seinfeld voice:* "What's the deal with socks, huh? Why do they disappear? And where do they go?" That was just in my bedroom, though, in front of my Cabbage Patch Kids and Pound Puppies. I never thought I could actually do it for real. Stand-up comics are the class clowns that everyone likes. That sure wasn't me.

"I don't know," I told my sister. "I don't think I could do that. What if I'm horrible? What if nobody laughs?"

"You can do this, Maggs, I know you can. You gave the best toast at my wedding."

She had a point. I did love giving that toast. I remember my opening line, spoken to my sister's fiancé. "We're so happy that you and my sister are getting married. Just always remember that there are no trade backs, she is yours now to deal with ... forever. Our job is done." That got a laugh, but it was in front of my family. Could I really tell jokes in front of strangers? So far my only other audiences were those Cabbage Patch Kids and the Pound Puppies, and even they were a tough crowd. I told her I would think about it.

At that point in my life my mind wasn't thinking about comedy. I was in a stable job and I wanted to go to graduate school for business. The following Tuesday I decided to go to an information session on how to prepare for the Graduate Management Admission Test. The GMAT is the test that's required when you apply for graduate school in business. I got the times wrong and ended up getting there an hour too soon. While I was waiting, I decided to walk around the neighborhood, and discovered that the coffee shop my sister told me about that ran the open mic was a few blocks away. The open mic was, in fact, just about to start. I called my sister, and she met me there.

The open mic was at a cozy coffee shop in the heart of Berkeley. There was a small room in the back, with some chairs facing a microphone. The MC was warming up the audience. As soon as we sat down, I immediately felt at home. I watched as each comic came up to do his or her seven-minute set. They were just ordinary people telling stories about their lives. I thought to myself, *I think I can do this.* I told my sister that the next week we were coming back, and that I'd have seven minutes of material ready to go. She was shocked at my certainty that I would be ready in one week, but supported the idea. The GMAT prep class would have to wait.

I was so excited to start writing, but what would I write about? Many comics make fun of other people. I didn't know if I could do that. I knew how much it hurt to be the butt of other people's jokes. Growing up tall, I would get teased about my appearance all the time. It sounds exciting to be tall, but as a child it was awful. I just wanted to look like everyone else. And I wasn't tall and skinny, like a model. I was tall and big. My sister would say, "You weren't fat, you were just *awkward.*"

There was an incident in elementary school that really affected me. When I was in fifth grade I decided to start a dog-walking business. I made fliers and put them in my neighbors' mailboxes, a magic marker drawing of me walking a dog. I had one neighbor who paid me three dollars to walk her dog around our neighborhood for half an hour.

One time I was walking the dog by some older boys in the neighborhood. I thought I looked pretty cute in my outfit of matching shirt and shorts from TJ Maxx. One of the boys yelled out to me, "Hey! Who's walking who?" Then they all laughed. I didn't really get it at first, but then, after thinking about it a while, I realized what they meant. They were trying to say that I was as ugly as a dog, so maybe the dog was walking me. Ouch. It shouldn't have been that big of a deal. Kids tease each other all the time. It's just a part of life. But it really affected me. I couldn't let it go. It really hurt, deep down.

Throughout my childhood, when I got teased or made fun of I had a hard time letting it go. I was pretty sensitive. I never wanted to make anyone else feel like that. So I made a decision to try not to make fun of other people in a mean way in my stand-up routines. Don't get me wrong; I didn't want to be totally clean. I just didn't want other people's pain to be the only source of my jokes. It seemed like that would create a lot of negative energy, no matter how many people laughed.

If I didn't make fun of others in my comedy routines, what would I write about? Ah yes—if I made fun of myself, then I would be in control. But what about me would I make fun of? I had to do some soul-searching. I wasn't ready to talk about my experience with bipolar disorder yet. I needed to find topics that were real, that other people could relate to. At the time I was single. It had been a year since I was in a serious relationship. I had all this pain and angst brewing inside of me about my love life. Dating had always been a painful issue, even from the beginning.

About eleven years earlier in eighth grade, at the age of fourteen, I got set up on a blind date, my first date ever. My good friend, who went to a different school, was talking on the phone one day with a guy named Bull. Doing what eighth-graders typically do, she impulsively handed me the phone to talk with him. We hit it off immediately. In the upcoming days we talked on the phone several times, and I would get these butterflies every time we did. One time I told him that I liked the group U2, and he said, "I like you ... too." Oh. I almost melted. Finally a boy was interested in me! I couldn't wait to meet him.

Bull and I decided to meet at Round Table pizza in town one Friday night. That was where all the scary cool kids from the public school hung out. I went to a small Catholic school, so teenagers intimidated me. I was so nervous. My dad dropped me off in our wood-paneled station wagon. I felt so alone. I walked into the restaurant, and it was full of teenagers who scared the crap out of me.

I didn't see anybody who looked like him. I walked around the whole restaurant, but no boy came up to me. I told him what I was going to be wearing. Where was he? Was I early? Was he late?

Then I saw my friend, and she had a very sad look on her face. I asked her where Bull was. She hesitated, and then said, "I am so sorry. He saw you and didn't want to meet you." My heart sank. I was devastated. He hated my appearance so much that he didn't want to even meet me? I got out of that scary teenage-infested Round Table as fast as I could. I wanted to die. I thought maybe it was because I was too fat. I needed to lose weight, I thought. I decided to try the whole anorexic thing. That lasted about three hours. I love food too much. I never got over that incident, though. It made me feel ugly and insecure about my appearance for many, many years.

When I started writing jokes, memories from those painful experiences came forward. Now, though, I could look at that overwhelming sense of loneliness with a different perspective. Perhaps I subconsciously tapped into that pain and frustration from my childhood. Jokes about my appearance, about my attempts to date, and about all the rejection started to emerge. Who hasn't felt lonely now and again? Who hasn't been rejected? Of course, the pain from my hospitalizations and diagnosis added to that raw emotion.

I saw each joke as a puzzle that I needed to put together. I would pick a situation in my life and just mull it over in my head. The cool thing was that I could write jokes while doing other things. The jokes were always in the back of my mind. As I would drive, or work, or wash dishes my brain was crafting a joke. It became my favorite thing to do.

Writing jokes became one of the best forms of therapy for me. I considered myself to be a somewhat anxious person. My mind was usually tied up with worrying. I would obsess about negative things, like bad decisions I had made, the reasons I was so unhappy, or potentially negative scenarios for the future. When I was manic my mind became my worst enemy—so many thoughts filled my head.

I couldn't control my racing mind. Now, with stand-up comedy, my brain was working for good. I would think of subjects and mull them around in my head until the punch line became clear. It gave me so much relief. Jokes became a sort of babysitter for my brain. If I was crafting a joke, my brain couldn't get into trouble by devolving into negative thinking. Comedy had consumed me and I loved every minute of it.

As I had planned the following week, I came back to the coffee shop in Berkeley with seven minutes of material. I was so nervous. The MC called my name and I walked up to the mic. I was trembling with fear. "What was I doing?" I thought to myself. But the other part of me was like, *I got this.* I went into my opener.

"So, this is my first time doing stand-up. But unlike another very important *first time*, this time I'm going to keep my eyes open the whole time, and I am not going to cry when it's over." There was a split second of silence, then *bam.* They laughed. They actually laughed! It felt amazing. It wasn't *at* me. It was *with* me.

Feeling confident, I proceeded with my next joke. I don't remember the exact wording, but it had something to do with the fact that I didn't look like my dad, but like the milkman. It fell flat. It didn't work, and there was silence. It was the most painful silence of my life. Oh, yuck. So this is what this feels like! I felt naked on that stage. I quickly went into my next joke.

"I've always been really tall. In fourth grade I was taller than my whole class. I couldn't fit into kid's clothes, so I had to shop in the adult women's section. So there were all the ten-year-old girls with cute dresses, and there was Maggie in the corner with her shoulder pads, gold buttons and Easy Spirit pumps." The room erupted with laughter. It was even bigger than the first joke. It was incredible.

I will never forget that set. I was immediately hooked on stand-up. It was like a drug and I had had my first hit. I didn't just like being on stage, I really enjoyed writing the jokes. The trial and error of figuring out the punch line until I got it just right.

Wordsmithing each line. Then being able to share this with others. Man, what a high. I felt good—and I hadn't felt good in a long time.

After the show, several of the comedians came up to me to tell me they liked my set. I couldn't believe the nice things they said to me. Well, that's not entirely true; part of me knew I could do this. However, I didn't feel like a *real* comedian yet.

I felt the same way about being referred to as a comedian as I did about being labeled a person with bipolar disorder. The title of comedian didn't seem to fit. I didn't feel funny enough to be considered a comedian. I had never been the class clown. I was still that insecure girl who stayed home alone on Friday nights.

However, my stint in that little coffeehouse was just the beginning. My career in comedy had begun.

# just business as usual

About seven months had gone by since my first comic performance. It was the winter of 2004. Things seemed to be going really well. I was twenty-six. It had been exactly ten years since my first hospitalization. I was in a good place. The year before I had struggled with depression after that seriously painful breakup. I was still doing stand-up comedy, which, surprisingly, was helping me work through that pain. A few months earlier in October I also left the law firm I'd been working at. I was now working as a representative for a media research company.

I felt like I was finally on my way. I was over the breakup. I not only had a job, but also a possible career. I had paid off all my credit cards, and except for my student loans, I was debt-free. I had a pretty normal life. I continued to take my medications regularly. I went to the gym a few times a week. My roommates and I would go out to the bars on the weekends, trying to find our next true love. Usually we'd end up finding a lot of alcohol and unavailable men. We had extraordinary dinner parties with new and interesting people we'd met in the Bay Area, drinking, dancing and laughing into the wee hours of the night.

I was taking a weekly class at the San Francisco Comedy College, which I absolutely loved. At this class I was learning the technical structure behind writing jokes from a skillful and seasoned professional comic. I was introduced to a whole new world that inspired me. I also made some great new friendships in this supportive comedy community. Stand-up became the most important thing in my life. Whenever I could get stage time I would take it, even if it were a tiny open mike. Every few months or so I had a big comedy show with the SF Comedy College and would invite my friends. My sister and her husband lived nearby, so I would spend time with them when I could. I really had things together, or so I thought.

I think it was the stand-up that made me feel particularly good. Like I felt when rowing on the crew team, when in a comedy club I couldn't get depressed. I was no longer that insecure and anxious, lonely and confused tall girl. On stage I was in control. Performing my routines almost healed something inside me. It wasn't that I *wanted* to do stand-up—I *had* to. For as long as I could remember I'd had all this stuff jammed up inside me, and now stand-up opened the door so it could all come out.

At first, I did get a little nervous before I had to perform, so I developed a technique to help with the nerves. Before each show, I would eat a big meal. The meal was so big that I would get very full, so full that my stomach hurt. I became so preoccupied with the stomachache that I totally forgot about the show. I discovered that nervousness evaporates when you're in pain. Then, once I went on stage, I could focus on the material. The pain of the stomachache would become overshadowed by the high of the crowd. Genius!

There was only one thing that got in the way of my stand-up; my job at the media research company. It started to take up more and more of my free time. I originally took the job because I really believed in the company, and the potential for me to advance was great. I was very excited about the new position and felt it was a perfect fit for me. As a bilingual membership representative, I introduced the company to new clients and then educated and trained them in the company's procedures. I spoke with

English-speaking and Spanish-speaking clients, an aspect of the job that I loved. Before I worked with clients, the company sent me to the East Coast for three weeks of training. I excelled in the training, earning the highest scores of my group. I got a brand new, shiny company car to drive around. I was set.

Unfortunately, the actual job was not what it had appeared to be. In addition to training new clients, something I enjoyed and did easily, I was also responsible for getting new clients to sign up for our services. Eventually I realized that the job was more of a sales position than an educational one. Client training was only a small part of the job; it was the signing of new clients I was judged on. We had weekly quotas that we were expected to meet, and meeting them was anything but easy. However, I am not someone who shies away from hard work. As a college student I'd held down a full-credit academic load and rowed on the crew team while also supervising the staff at the college Coffee House. But this type of work was different. Despite my superhuman efforts, I could not maintain the level of performance demanded of me.

As I became increasingly desperate to succeed, my job started to take over my life. I began to work nights and weekends, but it didn't matter how much work I put in; all that mattered were my numbers. Trying to succeed in a job that was really a full-time sales position was extraordinarily difficult. The stress was exacerbated by my immediate supervisor, who would regularly tell staff members how replaceable we were. She often reminded us that if we didn't meet our quotas we would lose our jobs. Despite working harder in this job than in any other I'd ever had, I still couldn't do it. I could not hit those quotas! Eventually I discovered that I wasn't the only one. Compared to my co-workers, I was, in fact, doing quite well. I was doing so well that the company sent me to Los Angeles for a few weeks to help in areas where others had failed.

More problems arose in late February when I requested to take off two weeks in the summer so that I could go to my brother's wedding.

His fiancée was French Canadian and most of her family was in France, so that's where the wedding was going to be. My family is very important to me, so missing that wedding was unthinkable. I adored my brother. Unfortunately, my boss would not approve my vacation until I met my quotas.

The stress that my supervisor put on her staff was unhealthy. From whispered conversations with co-workers I heard rumors that, based on the information we were able to utilize and the leads they gave us, the quotas were not reachable. I was stunned, and tried to stem my mounting anger. I started to feel like the Jack Lemmon character in *Glengarry Glen Ross,* wondering each day if I'd manage to earn a Cadillac Eldorado, steak knives, or a pink slip. The supervisor who each day threatened our jobs and livelihood started to seem like the Alex Baldwin character.

The thought of losing my job and of not being able to go to my brother's wedding started to really weigh me down. I began to obsess about my work. I started working more and more, late nights, Sundays, it didn't matter. I even started to compromise my values to get people to sign. If I noticed they were Christian, for example, I'd wear a necklace with a cross on it and drop a few religious words or phrases. I would pretend to care about people to get the sale. I felt awful about myself. This went against everything I stood for. The stress continued to get worse, and still my efforts were not enough.

I started to develop an intense anxiety around my work. Those of you who work in sales know that feeling, that pit in the bottom of your stomach when it's been too long since you scored a sale. The worry started to really take over my life. I was constantly strategizing and planning, and my left brain was working overtime.

I should have recognized the severity of the situation, considering that a similar one had caused my first two episodes ten years earlier. In high school, before I was hospitalized at sixteen, I had seriously overscheduled myself, creating an atmosphere of stress and tension that snowballed from overloaded to out of control. The honors classes, the three sports teams, the complicated research paper on Russian history, the sleepless nights: it was an explosive mix. The loneliness, low self-esteem, and anxiety only made it worse. All these circumstances sent me to the hospital at such a young age.

Now, almost exactly ten years later as an adult, I was in an eerily similar situation. I was working day and night, my self-esteem was low and my anxiety high as I fought and struggled, just trying to keep my job. I started getting less and less sleep. The whole situation was laying the groundwork for a big disaster. Dun, dun dun!

# the gym incident

In early spring 2004, March to be exact, I had two things going on in my life—my job and my stand-up. I also wished that there were a man in my life, but that was not happening. The last guy that I casually dated had given me the old "I'm not looking for anything serious right now." I, of course, told him I felt the same, as I was secretly deciding what color of flowers were going to be at our wedding. The desire to do stand-up got stronger and stronger as the stress of my job got more and more intense. I had to search for solutions. Giving up was never an option for me.

To be honest, it's not so much that my motto has been "Don't give up." It's been more along the lines of "Don't f- everything up, or people won't like you." I think I have always been trying to be enough for the world that I live in. I think most people do the same.

As I look back on my life, I can now see the extent to which "Failure is not an option" or "Don't f- it up" has helped to shape my life. The first job I ever had was at the age of fifteen, when I worked at a dog kennel where pets stayed while their owners vacationed. I started working there in my sophomore year. I got the job because I wanted to play with the dogs, and especially because I needed money to pay for my dress and limo ride for our high school's winter formal. It was a "girls ask guys" event. I worked at the dog kennel every Saturday morning from 8:00am to 12:00 noon.

It turned out that I wasn't going to play with the dogs, I was going to clean out their poopy kennels. Then for the last twenty minutes of the shift, I got to play with the dogs. This was not the job I was hoping for. Did I quit? No way, man. I put on those boots every Saturday and scrubbed that crusty dog poop off the floor and walls of the cages. Those kennels were sparkling when I was done—at least until the occupant returned.

I started working there in September and continued into the holiday season. Christmas Day was my favorite day of the whole year. I don't think I had ever been happier than I was on Christmas morning. It was a magical day for me, even in high school. Except for that year. That year, Christmas fell on a Saturday.

I talked to my boss and she said I had to work Christmas or I would be fired. Dogs don't stop pooping, even for Christmas. My parents wanted me to just quit. The winter formal had already passed, so it was far less important for me to work there. What? Quit? That wasn't an option. That morning, I put on the boots and scrubbed the magical Christmas doggie poop off the cement. I fed every animal and cleaned every cage. Luckily, Boss Scrooge allowed me to leave early. I missed Christmas breakfast, but my family waited for me to get home before we opened presents.

Basically, if I start something I'm going to finish it. There is no giving up. I have never quit a job without a really good reason. In college, when I rowed crew for four years there were many times I wanted to quit. In our novice year there were thirty of us that made the team. Rowing is a really hard sport to stick with; the 5:00am practices and crazy workouts caused many devoted rowers to put down their paddles. In our final year, out of the thirty that had made the team, only four of us were left.

My job in Argentina after college was even more challenging. It was a lot of fun, but almost too much work. As an English teacher working with a traveling school, we would go to a city and implement three- or four-day immersion programs. We worked a grueling schedule of mostly twelve-hour days. There was virtually no time off, the pay was low, and we had bare-bones accommodations. At the time, Argentina was also undergoing a lot of civil unrest. Riots in the streets were frequent. I wanted to come home so badly. But I stayed. I stuck it out until my contract ended.

So when I encountered the impossibly challenging media research job, I put on my armor and prepared to do battle. Just like in the past, failure was not an option. I was *not* going to fall apart. I was going to meet my quotas, go to my brother's wedding, and become a stand-up comic. End of story. But in order to do this, I knew that I needed to get rid of the stress.

The rising stress level was getting in the way of my being able to succeed at work. I decided to take a spiritual approach to the problem. I have always been a seeker—you know, the type of person searching for spiritual meaning. I was raised Catholic, but have always been very open to other approaches.

Over the years I had been obsessed with self-help and New Age books. Gary Zukav, Wayne Dyer, Iyanla Vanzant, Eckhart Tolle. These authors—some of my favorites—had comforted and educated me time and time again. Moreover, my faith in God has always been very strong. When I would go through major depressions, I would lean on my faith to get me through them. Going to church sometimes was the only thing that made me feel better. As a result, I decided that prayer and meditation were the best tools I could use to get out of this stressful situation. I was still on my medications, so what could go wrong?

I found a meditation CD to try in the morning and at night, as well as great CDs of motivational speakers to listen to during the day in the car while driving the many miles required for my job. Every morning I would do a meditation of at least thirty minutes. I would close my eyes, quiet my mind and chant "Ah" or "Om." Then I listened to motivational CDs as I drove to different locations during my workday, and meditated again in the evening before I went to bed. I would find success. I would be successful.

Then something cool seemed to happen. The meditation and the CDs seemed to help, a lot. I can't really describe it, but wonderful little coincidences started occurring. I would think something like "I wonder what so-and-so is doing right now," and then so-and-so would call me at that exact moment. I would worry about a certain detail about my job, and all of a sudden it would just resolve itself. If I needed something it would all of a sudden show up.

Then came those times at the store. As I was in the check-out line at the grocery store one day, the cashier gave me the total of what I had purchased, and when I emptied my wallet, I discovered that I had the exact amount in both bills and change, no more no less. I didn't think anything of it, until it happened again. I was always such a planner, and now it started to seem that I didn't have to do that anymore. Things just seemed to work themselves out.

Now I know you're thinking, "Well, those are just coincidences, Maggie." And I would agree with you. However, they all coincided perfectly with my newly developed spirituality. My budding belief system opened the door to the possibility that constant meditation and prayer and a regular dose of enlightening and positive literature could make my life better. The extraordinary coincidences started to happen more and more and more.

It all came to a head one night at the gym. I was walking on the elliptical machine at my fancy workout facility, listening to my Walkman (yes, I had a Walkman in 2004). The elliptical was on the second floor, positioned in a direction that allowed me to look down at the basketball court. I was jogging on the elliptical, gazing down onto the basketball court, and thinking about my life. And then it happened. A thought came to my mind. I wish I could remember exactly what it was, since this moment ended up being such a big one for me. What I do remember is that the thought became distilled down to a specific phrase, something like this, "Don't be afraid, you can do it."

The instant I thought of it, that phrase, verbatim, was sung in the song I was listening to on my Walkman radio. I slowed my pace a little on the elliptical, and considered this. It scared me a bit, but I thought, "Hey, it's just a coincidence. There's no way it means anything." I picked my pace up again, and as I returned my gaze to the basketball court, I saw something I hadn't noticed before. It was a banner, and it was hanging above the court. I hadn't paid any attention to it before, but now my eyes fixed on it, and when they did, I saw that the banner said: "Don't be afraid, you can do it." The exact phrase, word for word! It was as if the universe was trying to communicate with me.

It wasn't just this phrase that got to me. It was also the strong emotions that immediately took over me. This rush of adrenalin filled my body. Exhilaration, wonder and awe consumed me like I had just seen a ghost. My heart started pumping really fast. Then I freaked out, forgot how to use my legs and I fell off the elliptical. I quickly got up off the floor, grabbing for my Walkman and headphones, overcome with excitement and fear. Something had just happened. It felt like I had experienced another dimension, and I was feeling both thrilled and terrified. I went to the mat and tried to do some pushups to get my mind off what had just happened. My body felt light as a feather, and I did twenty with ease. It was as if I had superhuman strength.

I knew it was possible that I was having some sort of nervous breakdown, but it was confusing. What I was feeling fit in with so much of what I had read on peak experiences and spiritual awakenings. I knew it wasn't normal, but it was so exciting. I felt in my heart that what was happening was miraculous, and spiritual. I wanted so badly for this to be true, to go with the whole spiritual enlightenment thing. I was aware, of course, that there was the possibility that I could be on the verge of another episode, and believe me, this thought was beyond frightening. But that didn't feel totally right either. I had come so far. I wasn't that powerless girl anymore.

I decided to sleep on it. Either something really great—or really bad—was about to happen. I wished I knew which one it would be.

# next stop, manic episode. all aboard!

After the gym incident, I tried to continue with my life as if nothing had happened. I went to work and hung out with my friends, but I felt like I had this incredible secret inside me. It seemed like every day I would see more of those little coincidences, secret messages and signs that had no rational explanation. At first they *seemed* like coincidences. But after the gym incident I paid more attention to them, and they took on a deeper meaning. They felt more like signs that came from another dimension, or originated from another source, possibly even God. Being labeled crazy at such an early age, I often dreamed of being taken to a different world where I wasn't crazy. Where I belonged. I thought to myself, what if these signs and feelings might eventually lead me to a better place?

One day following the gym incident, I walked around Lake Merritt, and the beauty of the lake overwhelmed me. The colors were so vibrant! The water was magical; it glistened with a beautiful, radiant blue color that I'd never seen before. The grass surrounding it was a gorgeous green, lush and fresh. Now, if you have been to Lake Merritt in downtown Oakland, you'd have seen that it's nice, but not quite *that* nice. As I walked past people, I would look them in the eye and smile. Every moment was an opportunity to connect with people, and every connection brought me delight. There were certain people who automatically radiated joy and happiness. Children, especially, seemed to emit this fun, loving energy.

In those magical days, my emotions were so powerful and my mind was spilling over with thoughts, but I couldn't catch them fast enough to put them into words. These emotions were so indescribable that using metaphors or maxims to put these feelings into words seemed to help. One in particular that came often was "Rome wasn't built in a day." That maxim, in my mind, explained how big changes were coming, but they wouldn't come all at once. I needed to be patient as the transformation happened.

In addition, thanks to my Catholic upbringing, Bible stories started to pop into my head as well. Everything had a deeper meaning than before. I started to understand some of the really important parables that Jesus had used in order to talk to us, to interpret God's message. I discovered that his messages are so profound that our human brains can't even comprehend them, so parables help us understand them. For example, Jesus said that, "The Kingdom of God is within you." I had heard this quote for years but now I finally realized what he really meant. Let me tell you, he wasn't playing around. Everything I needed was inside of me. This parable helped me see how I could create my own kingdom of God, right there in Oakland.

Different people "felt" different to me. I couldn't see them with my eyes, but I "felt" them. Someone's energy would completely overtake me. Someone who was laid-back felt good to be around. However, there were certain people with nervous or even negative energy who were difficult to be around. Every once in a while there would be a man or woman I'd pass near the lake who had weird negative energy that I didn't like and found almost terrifying.

I remember the day that a plumber came to the house. I got a quick glimpse of the middle-aged man in his blue uniform. I immediately felt like something was wrong, that this was a person who could not be trusted. The feeling overwhelmed me. On the other hand, one of my roommates had a friend staying with us who gave me a positive, peaceful feeling. He was a hippie, a free thinker. There was something about him that I just loved. It was in no way romantic; it just felt so good to be in his presence.

Another person that felt good to be around was a fellow comedian. Up to this point, he was someone who had only been my friend. Before this I might have had a little crush on him. He was very funny, attractive and charismatic. However, my whole life I was used to having crushes on guys that weren't reciprocated. I mean, this guy was way out of my league. In my normal state, I had accepted completely that he was firmly in the friend zone. However, as I became manic I became fixated on him. Being around him felt so wonderful.

I started to believe he was more than a friend and that we were meant to be together. We went to lunch one time after the gym incident. When we got back to my house we sat in the living room. I felt like he, being the guy I was meant to be with, would understand my revelations. I did the best I could to describe all the great feelings and enlightenment that I was experiencing. I wanted him to be on the journey with me. I didn't tell him about my romantic feelings, yet. I knew that would come later. First, I needed him to understand where I was.

Years later he described my state. He said I was super excited about everything and that I was talking really fast. He saw me sort of spiraling up. He didn't really understand what I was talking about. Being the nice guy that he was, he was very supportive. But his support was in no way romantic, just the kind of support a friend would offer. The more we hung out the more I felt like he was the one, that in my new life we would be together. I kept this secret from him, but inside I was falling in love—or should I say I was falling in manic love with him.

In addition to this newfound love, the anxiety about my job that had dominated my life for the past several months just started to melt away. I realized that I didn't need to worry anymore, that things would just work out. That was just how the universe worked. Money was like energy, and whatever I gave away would come back to me. I handed twenty-dollar bills to homeless people, knowing I would get it back and more. I went to Nordstrom's and bought clothes that I couldn't afford. One of the things I bought was a pair of stretchy, light-blue corduroy pants. I remember it bringing me so much joy to wear those. Later on in the episode I went to a department store and spent hundreds of dollars on expensive make-up. I believed that it was important to do whatever I needed to feel good. I deserved it.

As the days edged on, I started to slowly slip out of my reality and into the new world I was creating in my mind.

As the mania progressed I started to have new revelations about life, and even about comedy. I started to "feel" the comedy. This was different than I usually approached it. I had always stuck to my set list, which means I would only do jokes I had written and practiced. I would never talk to the audience in extended ad-libs, or spontaneous riffs.

I remember doing stand-up comedy one night as I was just starting to get manic. I had been doing comedy for about seven months. That night was different than any other show I had done. I felt the energy of that room. I was so calm and so sure of myself. I didn't need to stuff myself with food and induce a stomachache to avoid feeling nervous. I got on stage and it just felt *good*. I instinctively knew what to say. The comedy energy surged through me. I had no fear. I was confident and excited, yet a calm peace came over me. An inner voice said, "I got this, I got this." In this new state of mind I knew that making this audience laugh would have a ripple of positive effect.

I looked out into the crowd. It was dark and the spotlight shone in my eyes. I put my hand up to block the light so I could speak to someone in the audience. I saw a couple sitting close together on the right side, a few rows back and close to the aisle. I made eye contact with them and spoke.

"Well, you look like a nice couple." They both smiled with embarrassment but were afraid to speak. "Don't worry," I said. "No one's going to hurt you. We're more afraid of you than you are of us." The audience laughed, and the two victims looked a little more comfortable. I continued.

"Are you a couple?" They both nodded. "Are you happy together?" They looked at each other, nodded, and smiled. I continued. "Seriously, like, really happy?" They smiled again, and this time the guy spoke.

"Yes, we really are." I paused for a moment, and then said the first thing that popped into my head.

"Gross ... that sounds awful." The crowd laughed. "Who wants to be happy these days? I'd much rather live alone ... letting the bitterness *slowly* eat away at my soul." The crowd laughed again, reading my sarcasm. Then I ended it. "You guys are weird, good luck with THAT life."

Despite my increasing manic state, on stage I felt at peace, connected to something bigger than me. I actually felt funny, and I think the audience perceived me to be as well. While on stage, I believed I was connected to another source or dimension more powerful than me. That night reinforced my manic delusions and taught me that while I functioned in this reality I could still connect to that other dimension. It was so interesting. It was a big turning point for me.

The most important part of this episode, or whatever you want to call what was happening to me, is that it took away the negative, self-hating thoughts. All the worry and all the anxiety were melting away. I didn't need to stress, I didn't need to plan. I just needed to "be," and everything would be taken care of. I looked in the mirror and saw a different person. I loved my appearance. I was beautiful and strong. Unstoppable.

The relief that this brought me cannot be described. For as long as I could remember, worry, self-hatred and anxiety had controlled my life. I was never good enough, never pretty enough, popular enough, cool enough, or smart enough. Throughout my entire life, I had been so critical of myself! So judgmental, always feeling like a failure. But this episode, this inexplicable, fantastic episode, made all those feelings go away. For the first time in my twenty-six-year history, I didn't need to sweat the small stuff. Things would just happen.

Songs on the radio came on that spoke to me. I would climb into my car, and whatever I would be thinking of at the time, a song would come on and repeat that thought back to me. The experience that had freaked me out at the gym was now a regular occurrence. I remember getting in the car a number of times and Tupac coming on, singing about how everything was going to be all right. It was like Tupac was talking to me from the grave.

There was one song I heard often that I really connected with. It was by a group called Los Lonely Boys. It was a beautiful song, and the lyrics were speaking specifically to me. In the song, they are singing to God about the difficulties of being human and asking him, "How far is heaven?" I could totally relate. The reality of life had seemed so difficult before, but things were about to change. The song seemed to come on every time I got in the car. It was God reassuring me that I wasn't alone, that my heaven was coming.

**Heaven**

*Save me from this prison*
*Lord help me get away*
*Cause only you can save me now*
*From this misery*
*Cause I've been lost in my own place*
*And I'm gettin' weary*

*How far is heaven*
*And I know I need to change*
*My ways of livin'*
*How far is heaven, Lord can you tell me*

*Cause I've been locked up way too long*
*In this crazy world, how far is heaven*
*I just keep on prayin' Lord*
*Just keep on livin', how far is heaven*
*Lord can you tell me, how far is heaven*
*I just got to know how far, how far is heaven*
*Lord can you tell me*

*Cause I know there's a better place*
*Than this place I'm livin', how far is heaven*
*So I just got to show some faith*
*And just keep on giving, how far is heaven*
*Lord can you tell me, how far is heaven*
*I just wanna know how far, how far is heaven*
*Lord can you tell me, how far is heaven*
*Cause I just gotta know how far*
*I just wanna know*

Like Los Lonely Boys, I wondered how close was I? When would I be going there? I had to be patient.

In some ways, I felt as if I were the main character in the film *The Truman Show.* Everything revolved around me. Everyone was an actor in the "reality" that I lived in. And like that character, Truman Burbank, I was also starting to question the reality that I had been enslaved to for twenty-six years. In a pivotal scene in the movie, a stage light falls out of the ceiling of the television set that is far above and well hidden. Truman looks at the "sky," wondering, why the heck would a stage light fall from the sky? A minute later a news report comes on, saying that the light fell from a passing plane. The news on the radio was created just for him, just like the songs on the radio that I was hearing were "playing" just for me. However, unlike the Truman show, in which a corporation and power-hungry director planned those radio segments, a friendly and loving God was trying to communicate with me. He was trying to help me see that this painful human reality was not my home.

Ultimately, Truman Burbank wanted to get out of his reality, even though it meant letting go of his family and friends. That is what I felt I was doing: trying to break through and get to a different place, my home with God. I was preparing for the trip, even if it meant leaving my family and friends. As the days went by, this secret life became more and more important, and reality became less and less.

I started to read *Conversations with God* by Neale Donald Walsch. The book is supposed to be a conversation that a man is having with God. I spent many hours reading this book, and on each page it felt as if God were speaking directly to *me*. The principles of the book correlated perfectly with my new visions. God was communicating with me, validating my beliefs, which in this state were constantly evolving.

This is where it starts to get difficult to explain how I was feeling. Kind of like trying to explain a dream. I didn't know exactly where God was taking me. I knew I was not going to die, but I felt the place he was leading me to was heaven. But how could that be? I had been taught my whole life that heaven is a place that good, moral people go, when they die. But I didn't feel like I was going to die. I started thinking then that heaven wasn't this place in the sky. You don't have to die to go there. Heaven was a type of existence that was possible. Almost like a utopian society. And in this society, we are powerful beyond our wildest dreams. We are all loving and kind, connected with the big G-O-D.

This heaven is similar to our world, but we get to design our lives and you don't have to worry about money, or anything else. Anything is possible. In this new world, I would get to choose what I did. I decided I was going to become famous, most likely via stand-up comedy. I would also be extremely wealthy. Money is energy. I could spend it, and whatever I spent would come back to me, because I was keeping energy flowing. Although I wasn't "there" yet, in this new world, I could practice this type of living now in this reality. The same principles of energy and love applied to all dimensions. Unfortunately, in my current reality, no one understood that. They seemed so caught up in the material world. However, in my new life, I would be with those like me, open to a new way of existing.

Eventually I could probably do things like Jesus did. I had faith as small as the mustard seed, and I was about to move mountains. I would transition fully into that dimension to be with Jesus and my other people. It was all fantastic, and really, well, *wondrous.*

Although I was incredibly excited about this transition, a small part of me was terrified. Everything that I knew was changing. And every once in while I would get pangs of fear. One minute I felt at peace and then all of a sudden I was extremely scared. Most important, the complete change hadn't happened yet. I was still in this reality. I didn't know if it was going to be days or weeks. I might have a long way to go, so I tried to be patient and let go of the fear. I needed to continue to play my part of "Maggie Newcomb" for a while. I could prepare for this change and focus on stand-up comedy. But I was still here, and I just needed to hold it together for a while longer.

I remember one night, a couple weeks after the incident at the gym, when all my friends decided to go dancing in the Castro. For readers not from San Francisco, the Castro is the gay district of San Francisco, or, as I like to call it, Gay Disneyland. I used to feel uncomfortable going to gay clubs, and here I am going to admit something *extremely* embarrassing: I used to be afraid of gay men. I know that's horrible, and believe me, I am way past that now. At the time, though, I was worried that gay men would take all the straight men, and then I would never have a boyfriend. Pretty ridiculous, huh? So the old me wouldn't be excited about dancing in the Castro. But in those days of my rising mania, I wasn't afraid of gay men anymore. I could see the beauty in everything, and now, especially, in gay men.

So my friends and I went to the club, a place that would usually cause me to feel very uncomfortable. But on that night, fear wasn't there. I was filled with acceptance, with love, and with peace. Gay men became wonderful, and fun. In my near-manic state, I believed that they were God's angels who were sent to teach us about life. Part of me still believes that.

That night my friends and I smiled and laughed as we danced and danced. We lost ourselves to funky techno pop beats of Madonna, Britney and Cher. Let me tell you, if you haven't danced to Madonna's song "Holiday" at a gay club, you haven't lived. I wasn't even drinking, but I felt like I was drunk. As Eliza says in the movie and play, *My Fair Lady*, I could have danced all night. I felt the music in my soul. I was dancing with angels, and I couldn't be happier.

# family intervention

It's hard to say whether I was sleeping much at all in those days after the gym incident. Just a few days without sleep for a bipolar person can aggravate or even cause a manic episode. Even though I probably wasn't sleeping very much and the mania was taking over, I still sounded normal. I was able to keep my ideas about this new life to myself. I didn't sound crazy—yet. I remembered what happened the last time I tried to explain these remarkable feelings to my friends and family and I didn't want that again.

As the days went on I started to become more and more delusional. I began to focus more on the stories in my head than on the reality that was around me. I was preparing for a new life, and I had started seeing my work, family and friends as distractions or obstacles that would get in the way of it.

It was like Laurence Fishburne from *The Matrix* was going to show up at any moment and ask me if I wanted to take the red pill or the blue pill. I would be leaving this world of limitation but entering a new one where my outrageous life dreams would be real. I could do anything I wanted, literally anything, and I would succeed. All the uncertainty I'd had for the majority of my life about my intelligence and my talent—that was all gone. It was the fate of another Maggie.

Stand-up comedy made me feel powerful and helped me get closer to my new life. Consequently, I believed stand-up comedy was my new destiny. I knew that I was on my way to becoming a famous and successful stand-up comic, somewhere. Yes, I know. How the heck was a comic with only fifteen minutes of material going to do that? Before I became manic I knew that I was okay at comedy but was not outstanding. I knew I adored doing it and felt very confident on stage, but I wasn't planning to quit my day job anytime soon.

For as long as I can remember, I have been an extremely practical person. I never had any illusions of the magnificent things that were coming my way. I followed the rules and did what was expected. I chose practical jobs and I saw them through to the end. For example, after I finished rowing in college, I became a rowing coach. When there weren't any job openings I asked a rowing school if I could wash their boats and help maintain them for free. A few weeks later they saw what a hard worker I was and hired me. I didn't have any grandiose dreams of being the next big rowing coach. I went about it very practically.

So it's really intriguing that after the mania started I decided that I should immediately quit my job and become a full time stand-up comedian. That just isn't something I would do. I mean, how would I make a living? I had no idea what I was doing. However, I felt it was something I *had* to do; there wasn't even another option. In my manic state, quitting my job would be the first step in building my new Rome and getting to that new life.

As my eagerness to begin my new career in comedy intensified, my hatred for my current job grew. I not only hated the job, but it was evil. My boss, especially, seemed to be particularly heinous. Later I realized that although she wasn't the most ethical person, she probably wasn't evil. But at that time, she, and the company, seemed to be inexcusably terrible. The anger and the hate started to brew. The more manic I got, the more I realized that I had to get out of that job. Everything it stood for represented what was wrong with the world. In my new life, I would be away from the job and away from that corruption.

At that point I was working with a therapist named Karen. Karen had been my family's therapist since my first episode ten years prior. Although she was in San Diego and I was in Oakland, I chose to continue my therapy sessions with her by phone. She knew me pretty well. She'd had a great impact on our family, and helped us get through many issues over the years. We had one of our phone sessions a few weeks after my manic period had begun. I couldn't wait to tell her my plan.

"So, I know this is a little sudden, but I've decided that I can't work with my company anymore." I was near bursting with excitement. "I'm ready to make the transition into a full-time comedian," I told her with confidence.

"Now Maggie, you're talking about sometime in the future, right? Not anytime soon," Karen replied, with a slight concern in her voice.

"No, I'm talking about this week. I'm ready to tell my boss that I'm leaving, and I can't do it anymore," I said.

There was a pause, then Karen replied, "Do you already have a job in comedy?"

"Not yet," I said, "but I just know that I'm going to be successful. This is going to happen. Stand-up is my calling."

I could almost hear Karen frowning on the other end of the line. "Maggie, I really don't think this is a good idea." There was a pause, and then, "Have you been taking your meds?"

My heart sank. Why wasn't she excited about my new life? "Yes, of course! This isn't what you think. I'm fine. I'm better than I've ever felt."

Karen responded, "I don't think you should quit your job until you have another job lined up. I don't think that stand-up comedy can support you."

"You just don't understand my plan."

Karen was starting to get frustrated with me. "Have you thought about looking into stable jobs in comedy, like … maybe you could work for Disney and be a character at the amusement park?"

What? I thought. Is she *crazy?* A character at Disneyland? That's the worst idea I had ever heard. I couldn't believe it. My therapist just didn't understand. The tension grew in our conversation as each of us started to get angry at the other. I realized this call was not going as planned, so I found a way to get off the phone. She wasn't on board, so I didn't need her in my life.

I decided to go over to my sister's house in Berkeley to tell her the good news. To be honest, part of me was a little nervous, but I knew I was doing what I was supposed to do. Fate was calling, and I was going to answer the phone. I was headed in the right direction.

After I arrived at my sister's place, I told her about my plan to quit my job and make the big leap. She was the one that got me started in stand-up, so I felt sure she'd be in agreement. When I told her, I saw the same concern on her face that I'd heard in the therapist's voice. It wasn't that she disagreed with me, but she looked at me like she saw something that made her afraid.

"Have you been taking your meds?"

"Yes," I snapped. "It's not what you think."

My sister persisted. "Have you been getting enough sleep?"

*"Yes."* Her fear was starting to make me a little nervous, and I began to doubt myself, just a bit. Was I really making the right decision?

She continued, and with a calm voice, said, "I think you need a little break. Some time off to slow down."

I trusted my sister more than anyone in the world. I considered her suggestion.

"Maybe take two weeks off before you quit your job," she encouraged.

I replied, "No, I can't stay with this company any more. I have to get out."

She reasoned with me. "Look, just do this for me. Give yourself some time to think." That was probably the best thing that my sister could have done for me. We sat there for a while as she slowly convinced me to take some time off.

I went to my car, called my boss, and left this message: "Hi, this is Maggie. I'm having a family emergency and I need to take two weeks off, starting now. I'm really sorry." It wasn't what I wanted, but at least I was free, for a bit.

That was probably the last rational decision I made at that time. The coming days would take me to a completely different place, one that was exciting, scary and very dangerous.

# down the rabbit hole

So my transition from a normally functioning person with mild mania to a manic person with mild psychosis quickly escalated. It was April, early spring, and in Northern California that means that a whole new crop of flowers was blooming. Bright yellow poppies and pink rhododendrons, and people are taking trips to Bodega Bay, Point Reyes and the San Francisco Botanical Gardens.

I, however, wasn't doing any of these. I was living in the environs of my newfound dreamland, and reality was fading away. I knew that soon I would be entering my new existence. I would be wildly successful. I would be united with a guy who I believed, at the time, was the love of my life. I would never have to worry about money again. I would feel confident and popular. I could walk into any situation and not be afraid or intimidated.

Above all, the most important part was that in this new life, I did not have a mental illness. In fact, everyone would see that I'd never *had* a mental illness. I had been normal all along. I wouldn't have to take medication anymore. I wouldn't feel ashamed. I would take off the emotional handcuffs that stopped me from being who I'd always wanted to be. I would be enough. I didn't have bipolar disorder, I wasn't flawed, and I would just be me.

Perhaps this new life and world I was stepping into was a result of all the sound decisions I had recently made. I had paid attention,

I had listened to my intuition, I had followed the signs, and I had let go of my past insecurities and worries. It also crossed my mind that I might be experiencing a form of the butterfly effect: something infinitesimally small had happened, but it was about to trigger a very big change in my life. This imminent shift in my life also reminded me of the movie *Sliding Doors.* In this film, a minor occurrence in the life of Helen, the central character, creates a rift in the time/space continuum, and her life splits into two alternate universes. I had experienced some subtle but profound occurrences, and I was about to step into an incredibly wonderful alternate universe, too. Except that I am not nearly as cool as Gwyneth Paltrow—I don't think anyone is.

A whirlwind of emotions and thoughts began to take over my brain and, eventually I could not control the storm. At first they were all exciting, fun thoughts, but scary, negative ones slowly crept in behind them.

Just the thought of my job continued to bring up all these raw, powerfully negative emotions. In retrospect, this is more evidence of the potentially dangerous nature of mania. Sometimes mania can create paranoia and angry emotions. Although I certainly had some valid claims, my anger with the company was beyond rational. I built conspiracy theories about it in my mind. The company had been around for several decades and had set some important standards in its field. I felt, though, that it was a corrupt, evil corporation, and it was destroying America! I would think about how awful they treated their employees, and I'd get enraged. At one point I wanted to call the head of the company and tell him "I know what you're doing, and you're not going to get away with it!" I wanted to be a whistleblower and save the world. The company had not been entirely upfront in its explanations of what was expected, but was it evil and destroying the country? Uh, probably not. At that point, though, it really didn't matter, because my intense dislike grew into hatred. This hatred that fueled my anger and indignation began to overpower me. Due to the mania, I couldn't see reality. My emotions clouded my judgment.

Although I was definitely not sharing the same reality as the rest of the world, others still couldn't tell, because I knew how to act. This was not my first episode. As I mentioned earlier, I knew only too well what happened when you shared your feelings of spiritual enlightenment and self-assurance with others. I knew better. You have to be quiet, you have to resist the urge to share what you're seeing and thinking and feeling, no matter how important it is to you. I knew how to fake being normal. I was not going back to the hospital.

However, after that phone call to my boss, my ability to fake it started to dissolve.

I spent the entire weekend in the house with my roommates. I remember making pancakes that Sunday morning. We sat in the living room and ate the delicious fluffy pancakes accompanied by red strawberries and sweet melons. The glowing light of the sun filled the room as we shared stories and laughed. I felt like I was getting closer, this house could be the portal to my new life.

Do you remember the scene in the movie *Beetlejuice* when the Alec Baldwin and Geena Davis characters come back to their house after they've died? They're freaked out and attempt to leave the house, but when they do, a door opens to a different world. The house is surrounded by sand, and there are sand monsters with big, toothy fangs swimming around them. They can't leave. That's how I felt about the house I was in. I couldn't leave it, but I was waiting for something or someone to take me to the other side, the new world, my *real* home—or maybe even heaven.

At night I would lie in bed, but I didn't sleep. I would be in my head, creating and recreating stories about my new life. One night, I believe it was the Sunday night of that weekend (I cannot be sure, because time is different in mania-land), I knew I needed to prepare for the crossover. I looked around my room and, one by one, anything that didn't match my new life I threw away in the trash. Any negative pictures and *anything* that related to my job. Only things that aligned with my new life and my new spiritual awakening could stay. I also threw away all my medications, an act I did not remember doing until someone told me so afterwards.

In a way, I can compare my actions to those of the members of Heaven's Gate or to any cult members who kill themselves, thinking that by doing so they'll be able to enter a new world. Those cult members believed that they must purge themselves of the stuff of their former lives if they wanted to enter their new one. I wasn't going to try to drink arsenic or catch a spaceship, but I did toss out the stuff in my life that didn't feel right anymore. I just *knew* that a big transition was about to take place.

The psychosis had started.

I believe it was the following morning that my roommates started to suspect that something was wrong. I was sitting on the sofa, looking at the orange I was eating. I looked closely at the peel of the orange and noticed that there were little dots in it. After looking at it for quite some time, I realized that the indented dots in the peel looked like the suction-cup "dots" of an octopus. How exciting! I was holding a beautiful little orange octopus, right there in my living room. So what do you do when you're holding something as magnificent as this? You talk to it, of course. Duh.

My roommate came into the room and sat on the arm of the couch, and started to look at me nervously. I think she may have seen me talking to the orange, my little orange octopus. She said to me, carefully, "Mags, are you okay?"

What a strange question, I thought. I kept looking at my orange cephalopod, and responded, "This orange color is so vibrant. Underwater the color looks different, though. Sometimes they don't swim very fast." I started enlightening her about the finer points of the orange octopus, not making much sense.

When I had finished, my roommate looked around the room nervously and said, "Have you talked to your sister lately?"

I looked over at her. When I did, the first thing I thought of was her grandma, whom I had met a few weeks earlier. What a great lady!

Then it hit me; this grandma was going to die at some point. My sweet roommate would have to suffer. I wanted to help her through this. I said to her, "Your grandma is going to be okay. She will be taken care of. Don't worry."

My roommate, obviously confused at the change of subject, was worried. On a side note, her grandma was in perfect health and wasn't about to die anytime soon. But she told me later that I was basically, "Talking like a crazy person, like you were the Tom Hanks character in *Castaway*, but instead of a volleyball, you were talking to an orange." I don't remember how long we talked. What we were talking about must have scared her, because minutes later my sister showed up.

Now I can't tell you everything that happened because I don't remember all the finer details, but I will give you some of the highlights that I can remember and what others have told me. It's difficult to be comprehensive when you are relaying what happened in a dream. I have fleshed out the story of what happened next by piecing together the perceptions and perspectives of my roommates, my family members and myself.

First, time had no meaning. My sister literally just appeared. She was a high school chemistry teacher at the time in Berkeley, which is about twenty minutes away. When my roommate called her at her school, she left immediately and came to be with me at our house in Oakland. The first thing she made me do was eat so that I could take my Lithium. She found the medication in the trash can in my room.

Then within minutes (or should I say manic minutes), my mom showed up. Now keep in mind that my mom lived in San Diego at the time. San Diego to Oakland is about an eight-hour drive, or an hour-and-a-half plane ride. The funny thing was that it wasn't weird to me, though, that my mom just appeared; I was more concerned about the things going on in my head. I must have sat on that couch all day while my family and roommates tried to figure out what to do with me.

They said that my body was there, but my mind wasn't. I would talk a lot about things, but I wasn't making a ton of sense. My family continued to try to get me to take my medications, hoping that this would bring me down. I'm told that I got upset with them, and occasionally yelled, "You're trying to poison me! Lithium is poison!"

My sister would assure me, saying, "Maggie, it's okay. We're not trying to poison you; we just want you to get better." I could understand her, in a thick, dreamlike sort of way, but I was so distracted by intense emotions.

My sister told me that I would get really excited one minute and then start to cry the next. Occasionally I'd slip into baby talk. Now that's just weird.

Here is a scene of my sister and I talking that reveals how I was acting. The two of us were sitting in the living room. My mother and roommates were in the kitchen. I would not stop talking about one of my roommates and her new boyfriend. I stared into space and said, "Their love is so pure. I mean, they're meant to be together. They each bring a part of their soul to the other. They are healing each other every day the more they love each other." I went on and on. I was filled with such intense emotion that my sister, not wanting me to get too emotional, would invariably find a way to bring me back.

"Maggie, look. We have some food here for you." My train of thought stopped. I looked at my sister, but for some reason started thinking about our father.

"Dad ..." I said, and started to tear up.

"What about dad?" my sister asked.

I lamented dramatically, "He is sick, he is very sick, he is dying." I started crying. My sister distracted me again.

"Mags, look out the window at all the pretty flowers." I looked out the window and saw the gardeners working. They were all Latino, possibly immigrants. I immediately felt sadness for them. They represented all immigrants who worked so hard and were treated so poorly. I felt this pain for them, and for their families. I felt the hard work that they had to do their whole lives, just to survive. I put my hand on the window and cried, "It's not fair."

"Maggie," my sister called out again. "Look—we got you some pizza. Your favorite: pepperoni, olives and pineapple. Let's just sit here and eat this. It's time to relax." She was able to distract me so that I could eat and take my medication. There was only one problem; the Lithium wasn't really working anymore.

I would go up and down in an instant. One minute I would I ramble on about certain people and one minute be crying, and the next minute feel intense joy. One of my other roommates in particular made me really upset. My roommate that caught me talking to the orange was fine. However, there was something about my other roommate, who was a very close friend from college, that made me so angry. She told me later that I said some very strange things just to her. Around the same time that I was in the living room I said to her, "You are like me. We are on a different level than everyone else here. Only some of us have this *knowing*. We have special abilities." The more I talked with her the more frustrated I got.

"You have the knowing," I chastised her, "but you aren't using it right. You aren't following the signs; you aren't listening to your soul!" Then I got pissed. "You're ruining everything!"

She told me that another time I yelled at her when she walked into the room. "Get out of here! I don't want YOU here. You know what you're doing ... you know what you are doing!" My poor friend had no other choice but to stay away; she couldn't reason with me. Keep in mind, she was one of my best friends from college. Her friendship was—is—so important to me. I would never yell at her like that.

I remember being irritated with that roommate, but I don't remember those details of me yelling at her. I think I was annoyed that my family and friends couldn't feel what I was feeling. If they could, they wouldn't be concerned with my medication or trying to change me. A small part of me knew they were trying to help me, but their energy bothered me. They were getting in the way of my new life starting. Although we were all in the same house, they felt so far away.

At this point my family was almost in panic mode. They didn't know what to do. They didn't have an actual psychiatrist to talk with. I had stopped seeing a psychiatrist about a year earlier and was getting my medications from my primary-care doctor. My sister called that doctor, but since she was not a psychiatrist, she wasn't extremely helpful. My therapist couldn't prescribe medication and was in San Diego, so she wasn't much help either.

All the while I kept telling them, "I'm fine!" And then I would plead with them, "Please don't take me to the hospital! I don't want to go to the hospital." I begged my sister not to take me there. I was adamant about not going. After what I had been through ten years earlier, that was the last place I wanted to be.

She'd respond, "Okay, relax. We're not going anywhere. It's okay." Unfortunately, deep inside, though, she knew that they might not have a choice.

*Now What?*

With horrible memories of the mental hospital at the age of sixteen looming in my head, I was absolutely positive that I didn't want to repeat that experience. My family and friends, however, did not share my certainty. Still at our Oakland house, the people closest to me in the world were trying to determine the best course to take for me.

That's when my sister and my mom had an idea: they would take me to my aunt's house, who lived well outside of the city. They thought if they got me out of my element and into the peaceful country, there was a good chance that I might snap out and come back to reality.

The past few days had taken a toll on my friends. The only Maggie that they had known for the past ten years was the stable Maggie. This new Maggie, the manic, psychotic one, was very frightening for them. They said that this new person looked like me, but it wasn't me. Even though they understood the technicalities of what seemed to be happening to me, they were afraid that I was gone forever. After my mother and sister took me out of the house, they all went out to dinner to talk about it. I was told that there were some tears shed. Not knowing what would happen to me was overwhelming for them.

I spent the next night at my sister's apartment in Berkeley with my mom and my sister. The following day we drove to my aunt's house, in a quiet town about 50 minutes outside of San Francisco. My aunt and uncle's beautiful house was surrounded by flowers and trees, with golden, rolling hills in the background. They were so generous to take us in. Like my mother, my aunt is also beautiful, with a great sense of humor and a love for life. Their four kids, my cousins, were all grown and out of the house.

Although I was full-blown manic by this time, I could, surprisingly, still keep it together when around new people that weren't my roommates, my mom or my sister. I could keep quiet when necessary and just observe what was going on, like I was watching a show on television. Although I may have looked normal, I was in a very strange place. Nothing around me seemed real. I was capable of speaking, but only about a few topics.

I remember having some great discussions with my aunt. I talked about the successful career in stand-up I was beginning, as well as telling her about my new relationship with the man of my dreams. I told her how terrific this guy was, a guy who, in reality, was just a friend, but in my mind was my future husband. I talked about how magical it was to perform stand-up on stage. I talked about writing jokes, how to be comfortable on stage, and how to speak to a large crowd. I also talked about how awful my job was. It is very interesting that in my condition I could have these, what I recall, profound conversations about philosophy, religion and spirituality. I could go on and on about these topics with ease. I was delighted at my new thoughtful insights.

Although I could talk at length about philosophy and enlightenment with my aunt, I couldn't take care of myself. As one area of my brain lit up with energy, other parts refused to work. I couldn't do simple tasks. I couldn't function on my own. I didn't know what day it was. I didn't know what time it was. I didn't think about eating. I didn't even know how to bathe myself.

At my aunt's house my sister had to help me take a shower, because like my first manic episode, I didn't know how to do it anymore. Seriously, the shower was like this foreign entity that made no sense to me.

I remember that we were both standing in the bathroom, and I stood there just looking at the shower, having no idea of what to do next. The shower almost scared me. I looked at my sister with confusion. She could tell that I wasn't going to do this on my own. She turned on the water and said, "Okay now, take off your clothes." I awkwardly did that and waited to hear what was next. "It's okay, now get in the shower." She went on. I got in the shower, but avoided the water. I looked at her still not knowing what to do next. "It's okay," she repeated. "You can do this. Get under the water. Take the soap and put it on your body." I moved under the water feeling very uncomfortable and still confused. She said "Maggie, now do this." She pretended to put soap on her body and scrub it on her arms and legs. I took the soap and followed her lead. "Good," she said. "Now, get it under your arms. Your legs. Okay, now put the soap down and rinse off … all the way off. There is still some soap on your shoulder. Good job." Then she turned off the water and gave me a towel. She helped me dry off and showed me which clothes to put on.

Unfortunately, staying at my aunt's house did not help. I just became more irritated because my family was getting in the way of me starting my new life. I was annoyed, but still overwhelmed by heightened sensations and emotions. The colors of the country were magnificent. When I walked outside, the gardens almost sparkled because the colors were so intense. I could hear birds chirping and see butterflies hovering over the flowers. Their dog was like an angel. In fact, I thought the dog was my old dog, Wilson, coming to be with me.

They increased my Lithium and gave me Ambien at night, but it wasn't enough. I would go to bed, but I wasn't really sleeping. My mind was still working overtime. I was in and out of delusions all night.

After a few days at my aunt's house, my mom decided that the best thing for me would be to go home to San Diego so that she could take care of me. I did not like this idea. It was another obstacle that got in my way. I had no problem voicing my concerns to my family.

"I don't want to go home!"

"Margaret," my mom pleaded, "it's the only option right now. Your sister needs to go to work and we can't stay here forever. Once you get home you'll feel much better."

I was furious. "I don't need anyone to take care of me! I'm fine. You don't understand."

My mom was patient with me. "I know, Margaret. Let's just take it day by day."

I was pretty detached from reality at that point. Time and logistics meant nothing to me. I was mad at my family, and I didn't really understand what was happening. I was angry and I was going to show it. I was mean and rude to my mom for the majority of the trip, and I didn't care what anyone thought of me. My mother was able to convince the airline to let us pre-board due to my unstable condition. My mom is a freaking saint. I am so blessed that she put up with me when I was acting so awfully.

We arrived in San Diego, and my other aunt, who lived there, picked us up from the airport. For some reason I was livid that she had picked us up. I didn't want to see anyone else that we knew. We got home, back in the house I grew up in and were greeted by my dad. He had Parkinson's disease, and he was starting to show signs of dementia. He tried to help with my situation, but the disease had already taken much of his strength and focus. He ate and talked with us, and tried to encourage me to get better. He was physically there, but it was my mom who dealt with me the most.

After we got to San Diego, I became more and more frustrated. My sister was able to work with me a little better than my mom was. My sister knew better than to argue with my delusions. When I would rant about my dreams and my new reality, my sister just distracted me or diverted my attention. My mom still tried to reason with me. Take it from me, when people are manic, there is no talking sense into them. I was in a different place, and the only way to get me out of it was with better medication, serious professional help and time.

I was tired of all the interventions. I felt that my mom, especially, had taken me away from my life in Oakland and had gotten in the way of my dreams. I was going to make the transition to my new life, and she had gotten in the way. She was to blame for my still being in this reality, a reality full of pain and suffering.

Upset and seething with frustration, I needed to vent, but even in that state I didn't want to harm anyone or anything. So I went outside and found our biggest shovel. I headed to the backyard near the trees and bushes where there was no lawn. I stuck the shovel into the dirt as far as it would go. I even stepped on it with all my weight so that the entire shovel was deep into the ground. I pushed down on the handle and pulled up the dirt to reveal a beautiful hole. I moved on and started digging more holes. I dug one hole, then moved on to another. I made little holes all over the yard, and with each hole felt a little bit better. I also picked the flower buds off of the plants. My mom watched me from the kitchen with confusion and compassion.

After only being home for about a day, things escalated very quickly. I can't really describe what happened next. A bad drug trip might be the best comparison. I remember sitting in the backyard. I felt like my parents were holding me hostage at their house, and I was furious. The sad thing was that I was suffering so much I couldn't see that they were trying their best to help me get better.

As I lay there on the pavement in my parent's backyard, my mood shifted from anger to fear. Images began to play before my eyes, freakish visions that seemed to invade my consciousness, almost as if I were being haunted by them. I was having grotesque delusions of my own death. The images, parts of which seemed to include flashes of horrible, violent moments from some *other life* sprang up and intensified. I watched in horror as I saw myself dying in front of my family's house.

Physical sensations were heightened and I became aware of the cold pavement on my skin. Suddenly an intense pain seized my body, and I was gasping for breath. I was overtaken with extreme panic and helplessness. Then my focus expanded and I imagined that firefighters and paramedics were bending over me and treating me, all of them moving in slow motion. They seemed to be talking but I couldn't hear anything, and my body was filled with fear.

All I could think was, I have to leave here, get out of my parents' house. But where would I go? I wasn't sure if I needed to call an ambulance. This pain that I was feeling: was it real? I was drenched in panic, and convinced that something bad, something awful, was about to happen.

The last thing I remember, I somehow got up off the ground and went inside the house. My dad must have said something to me I didn't like because I remember yelling at him for some reason. Then I ran outside to the front yard. I don't remember the next few events. This is what my best friend relayed to me. My mom was extremely distraught at my behavior and didn't know how to help me. She called my best friend and her mom, who live near my parents' house, and asked them to come and help her.

When my friend and her mom arrived, I was outside pacing in front of the house. My friend's mom came over to me. She gave me a hug, and I collapsed in her arms.

I remember waking up on the ground with my best friend and her mom bent over me. They were extremely calm and warm. My friend's mom, who is also one my mom's closest friends, smiled down at me.

"Let's go for a ride in the car," she said. They helped me up and we got into the back seat of the car. My mom was behind the wheel. My best friend and her mother each sat on one side of me, their arms locked with mine so I couldn't move.

They were taking me to the hospital.

# part 2 | GOD'S WAITING ROOM AND BEYOND

# the hospital of transition

It was springtime in 2004, the last day in April, to be exact. We pulled into the parking lot next to the hospital's emergency-room entrance on a perfect, sunlit day. Beautiful plants, blooming flowers and green grass surrounded the hospital. Although I had been protesting for days, saying that I didn't want to go to the hospital, this time I didn't put up a fight. I was done arguing with my family. I was tired. I sat in the middle seat with my best friend on my left and her mom on my right. Driving the car was my mom, who kept an eye on us in the rearview mirror.

I was starting to lose faith in the belief that I was about to transition into a new life or enter a new dimension, my heaven. Why hadn't it happened yet? Why was I still here?

We got out of the car. I looked around, and something about this location felt familiar. I knew this place. I looked at the sign. It read *Tri-City Hospital.* I immediately realized where I was. It was the hospital where I was born.

All of a sudden it hit me: I was going to be reborn in this hospital, the same hospital where I entered this world! It all made sense; I would make the transition into my new life at the place that had started this one. Why hadn't I thought of this before? I mean, it seemed so clear, right? I couldn't exactly just vanish into thin air. Maybe there was some sort of wormhole in this building. You know, those wormholes that you see on a science fiction series like *Star Trek*. Maybe this was the wormhole that I came from, and I was just going back home. Yes, of course! The more I thought about it, the more convinced I became. I had tried this little human experiment and now it was time for me to go back home. My work here was done.

I started to get excited. I was finally safe, and it was only a matter of time before I would start my new life. All the pain and suffering of this life would be over. I felt such relief. I knew that the people around me thought I was manic, but I didn't care. Manic, schmanic, I was starting over. I was pretty sure that God or angels were watching me in awe and preparing for my arrival.

We sat in the lobby of the emergency room for hours. I didn't mind the wait. Time didn't matter anymore. What mattered was that I was there. My friend told me later that I was very calm and talked about how I was going to become a professional comedian on a cruise ship. She said that I wasn't acting quite like myself. She could see a difference in my eyes. They were not normal; they looked *different*. She also said that I told her that I'd had conversations with Einstein, Teddy Roosevelt and Sigmund Freud. She felt that was kind of odd, but she knew not to argue with me. I don't remember specifically talking about these men with her, but I do remember having vivid dreams about them. I felt very close to Einstein and his theories. In fact, I felt that I was just following in his footsteps, uncovering the mysteries of the cosmos. In my manic state, string theory seemed so real and so basic.

After hours of waiting, I was finally taken back into a room to be examined. My mother and friends came with me. While walking through the halls I looked into a room and saw a man in a hospital bed. The man was handcuffed to the bed and there was a policeman standing outside his room. For a split second I got scared. It pulled me out of the fantasy I was in. Wait, what am I doing? Then this calm took over me. Something deep down inside me said to myself, "This is your destiny Maggie, just keep going. Rome wasn't built in a day. Don't question this." Then I came back to my journey and the manic feelings. I was almost there. I had to keep the faith.

In the exam room, I lay on the bed and my mom and my friends sat in there with me as we waited for the doctor. They said that I was very calm and told jokes. They were surprised about how upbeat I was, considering the circumstances. The nurse came in to take my vitals and left. My friend told me that after she left I said to her, "I don't think she understands what we're doing here." Then I smiled at my friend. She was worried, but she tried not to show it.

I remember lying on the bed waiting for the doctor, strategizing how this transition was going to go down. I thought, maybe the doctor will come in and give me a shot, I'll close my eyes, and then boom—open my eyes and wake up in a new place! I decided to close my eyes and see what happened. I closed them, and my world went black. I waited a second or two. Then I opened them. Nothing. I was still in that exam room with my family. Hmm, I thought, maybe I have to get away from my family to make the transition. They are probably holding me back.

The emergency room psychiatrist finally came in, and I talked to her alone. I remember thinking that I needed to convince her that it was my family's fault that I was in there. I talked at length about the past few weeks and how stressful things were. I probably wasn't making much sense. Since I was so manic it was difficult to explain anything with clarity. When you're manic, stories have no beginning or end. Telling them is akin to verbal diarrhea, accompanied by strong emotions. I just remember the psychiatrist nodding her head. For a brief moment, she looked at me with total compassion. Even in my manic state, I could tell that she wanted to help me.

Whatever I said or whatever my condition looked like must have been bad, because I was immediately admitted to the psych ward of the hospital. I said goodbye to my family and friends. At that point it was nighttime. We had waited all day just for me to be admitted. The doctor walked me over to the high-security section of the psych ward. The hospital first places all new psych patients there. Then, after a few days of observation, they move them to the low-security area.

Before they took me to my room, I had to sit with a woman to do an intake form. I really enjoyed sitting with her and answering her questions. I was in such a good mood. I was so excited to get away from my family. They were the last things holding me back. I had made it.

After the interview they gave me new medications to take. I didn't mind at all. These little pills had no real power over me or the universe. I just went along with the program. I knew my time would come. They showed me to my room. I noticed that I had a roommate, but she was already asleep. I climbed into my bed with my clothes on. I was still wearing my light-blue corduroy pants. The medication was extremely sedating. I completely passed out. It was the first time I had really slept in days, maybe even weeks.

# making sense of heaven

I thought that I might make my transition on the first night, but it
didn't happen. I must have slept more than fifteen hours, because
I woke up in the middle of the next day. I felt extremely refreshed.
I walked out of my room and into the main room of the ward. In
this main room was an open area with a long table and a few smaller
tables next to it where people could sit or eat. Next to the tables was a
large hangout area with sofas, a television, and coffee tables. A sliding
glass door led to an outdoor patio, a grassy area encircled by shrubs
and flowers. There was, of course, a high fence that enclosed the
garden, and the parking lot was on the other side of the fence. Our
bedrooms were near the main room. We could hang out in the main
room or in our own rooms, but there were only certain times that we
could be in the garden.

I was very excited about my soon-to-be transition but was also
strangely at peace. I figured I was probably in a sort of lobby area or
anteroom of heaven. I decided to think of it as God's Waiting Room.
This is where this whole book got started. It may have looked like an
ordinary room, but to me it was a magical portal. It was as if I were at
the pearly white gates of heaven and they were going to let me in as
soon as they finished preparing for my arrival. All the work was done.
I was already connected with this new heavenly spirit world. It was

like I was at Disneyland waiting in line to get on Space Mountain. I had arrived and I felt so close.

I needed to be patient. I might need to stay in this place until I was ready to cross over, but the transition was happening. I wasn't hoping, I wasn't dreaming, I *knew*. All my life up to that point had been a series of mistakes. The manic enlightenment was the vehicle that was taking me home again to where I belonged. Where we all belong, to be the best versions of ourselves. All of us patients were special like this. In our new heavenly lives we would have cool powers. We were like magicians and sorceresses with secret abilities.

I sat down at the main table. I remember one of the first things they gave me was a menu, so that I could choose my meals for the next few days. I stared at the menu. It looked like a blur of letters. When manic I had trouble reading. I could not focus on specific topics. I could write, but I had trouble reading. My normal self would have analyzed the menu, thinking hard about what I should be eating. Only the most healthy and balanced choices. But I was not my normal self. I looked at the menu again. It looked blurry. Then some random words popped out at me. Okay, I thought, and circled them. Some more words jumped out, and I circled them too. Anything that I saw that looked yummy, well, I just circled it. Pudding—yes! Cereal—why not? Chicken—sounds great! It was the new carefree Maggie, and everything was good.

In the high-security wing there were just a handful of characters with me. As I moved around this area or God's Waiting Room, I observed and analyzed the people. The staff would provide those who smoked with a cigarette when they went outside. I didn't smoke, but would often take one anyway and smoke it. It felt good, so I went with it.

We would also have meetings a couple times a day. They were simple meetings about confidence or friendship, the kind of enrichment classes they teach in grade school. A few of the patients would sit at the table, and there would be a person there to facilitate the discussion. Sometime it would be an inspirational reading, and we had to talk about how it made us feel. These meetings seemed beneath me, almost an insult. I mean, I had already figured things out. People should be reading articles that I wrote. (I call this the manic ego, by the way.)

The staff was pretty unremarkable. I found them to be friendly-ish but detached, which was fine with me. About every hour one of the staff members would approach and ask me in a bored voice two questions: Was I hearing any voices? I would say no. Was I having delusions? I would say no. Then they'd leave. Wow, what keen investigative skills.

The staff of the hospital reminded me of suburban moms stuck on yard duty watching other people's kids. They don't really want to be there and don't particularly care what the kids are doing; they just want to make sure no one gets hurt. While they were watching us they'd carry on conversations with each other, talking about us as if we weren't there, and as if they could not care less if we were.

Although for the most part I was pretty content, I was getting a bit impatient. I spent a lot of time in the garden, pacing back and forth. I ruminated on the new comedy and speaking career I would have in my next life, practicing sets and speeches in my head. I was going to be famous.

I knew the other patients like me were special. Society gave us a label of mentally ill, but we weren't sick. People with a mental illness like bipolar disorder were misunderstood by the human race. I was there with other mentally ill, magical beings to learn our craft. We were kind of like the mutants in the *X-Men* movies or for those purists, the comic books. This was our school to learn our talents, whether time travel, reading minds, or whatever. We had the power. Maybe once we perfected our magical abilities we would be going to a different place where people like us would be appreciated.

I had all these "revelations," and I couldn't believe how amazing they were! The magic was all around and in and through us, and people had to know about it! I thought to myself, this must be what

Einstein and Emerson felt. I decided that I needed to write these insights down. I wrote on napkins, the dinner menu, anything I could get my hands on. I wrote and I wrote. Thoughts would pop into my head and I would write them as quickly as I could. I could barely keep up. Wherever it was that I was going, I knew that these writings would be part of a bestselling book that would blow everyone away.

I saved all my manic writings. I don't really understand what they mean anymore. They aren't even complete thoughts. Here are a few of them. I'll let you be the judge.

- *Story: Truth behind every feeling, Body knows that feeling, Physical body pain wants to understand that principle = why bipolar people go through mania.*
- *Manics are drawn to people that will evoke you to express the feeling you need to heal.*
- *Everything you do is "inspired" by God.*
- *Father, son and holy spirit: you always have these 3, but in the presence of others you feel more of the father, son or holy spirit than they allow you to feel.*
- *Bipolar – You see God through other people's "eyes."*
- *If 2 people feel each other's "truth" then they will "let" you feel their "truth."*
- *You are drawn to those whom you think you need to "feel" their "truth."*
- *If you don't understand yourself—you don't understand your true feelings or true love—then it is more difficult to understand other people.*
- *You don't live your life in "earth" time. You live your life in your feeling time.*
- *Comedy inspires me because it is the opposite of pain. A good comedian "understands" pain so they can express it to people on stage in a way that will make them laugh.*

- *Bipolar people are no different than anyone else. Bipolar is just a man-made label for something we don't understand.*
- *Bipolar people don't know how to live in society's "time." Living in the world for bipolars is like putting them in an invisible box.*
- *Bipolars want to live in God's time which is through their instinct, inspiration and emotion.*
- *Since instinct comes and goes it's hard to determine when to act on that instinct since "society" acts mostly on human time restraints.*
- *I am the product of a brilliant lefter and a brilliant righter. It is difficult to know where to focus my energy when my instincts are so diverse.*
- *I am drawn to many and many are drawn to me because I allow God in.*
- *Why do we speak to children in a different tone with different words? We either understand they are children and won't understand adult language and terminology or we love the "child" and need to tell them in a way they will understand and won't be afraid of.*
- *While I am here in the "hospital" my mind has no concept of time, but it's easy to keep my mind occupied when there are no time limits.*
- *My speaking timing got "too fast" due to comedy.*
- *To write a joke you must know the answer.*
- *While writing I hear more than people want me to hear.*
- *I am reading body language and the pattern of questions mixed with emotional tone and body language.*
- *I only hear jokes and joke tone.*
- *Manic – body on different speed.*
- *Bipolar = Groundhog's day X 1 million—I can see all the possibilities, the different dimensions.*
- *Groundhog's day X 1 million—it was like the butterfly effect.*
- *Some manics can control which "feelings" they want to listen to, but it's difficult. It's like doing 1 million things at once and tuning 1 thing out.*

- *I sense emotions of others so I can adjust my attitude.*
- *It is very difficult for me to talk to people who are not "like" me, comfortable with self and God. I have to struggle to hear them talk, since they aren't showing emotion and are blocking mine. When people don't let you in and you have to struggle to "hear" them, it's exhausting on your body.*
- *Mania = term when you listen to your inspiration.*
- *Bipolar people—speak in code.*
- *When more than 2 "people" are gathered in my name—know that you are loved.*
- *If you only knew who walked beside you, you would never be afraid.*

When I wrote these, they seemed so important, so obvious. Now when I look at them they have lost that intelligibility, that magic. I find them interesting and slightly familiar. It's kind of like remembering a dream. It seems so clear, then in a blink of an eye, it's gone. You don't remember any of the dream anymore. Maybe someday all of what I wrote will be clear to me again.

I felt like I could write forever. I realized that time didn't exist for me as it had in the past. One day for me could be an hour in real time. What this meant was that I could write a bestselling novel or a masterpiece in a few days. I would be "in the zone." Time could stop or speed up at any time, and I had the power to control it. I was in that creative zone, and nothing was going to stop me. Pretty sweet, right? It wasn't as if I had only one hour to do something; the process would take as long as it needed.

Even though I was in a hospital, this creative zone felt like heaven. I started rethink this idea of heaven. More details about it came to me. I started to think that maybe heaven is not a place at all. It is an existence; it is a different layer of our own world, a layer that most humans cannot see. Heaven could be right where I am—it is a feeling and a presence. I started to realize that maybe we don't go anywhere when we die. Perhaps we shift into another dimension, a dimension that's already here. We shift there not for a moment like I had been experiencing the past few weeks, but for a lifetime. Only others like me could understand such a complicated idea, and soon I would be with those others. A community of people working together in harmony. Expressing ourselves through art.

In those first few days of the hospital one of my favorite times was mealtime, and it wasn't because of the main entrees. It was the pudding that came with them. The delectable, decadent and delightful chocolate pudding cups. It wasn't homemade pudding from scratch; it was just your everyday Jell-O pudding cups. Actually, I don't even think it was the Jell-O brand. It was some imitation or store-brand chocolate pudding cup. In my normal state I would never buy pudding cups for myself. They were a waste of money, not to mention unhealthy. It was an indulgence that I rarely experienced. Don't get me wrong, I love pudding. I mean, who doesn't? I used to love to make it as a kid from a mix. Just add milk, and in a few minutes it was ready. I especially loved eating the parts of the pudding that weren't mixed in properly, so it was a little thick or even had lumps. That was the best. As I grew older, I ate less and less pudding. I stuck to healthier options.

Now here I was, an adult, experiencing this imitation pudding cup as if it were the best thing I had ever tasted. It probably didn't even contain dairy or even real chocolate. But it didn't matter to me. It tasted like the richest, creamiest chocolate dessert I had ever had. I savored every bite. The smooth creamy pudding filled my mouth and my taste buds rejoiced in the rich chocolate flavor. It took me out of the hospital and into a *Charlie and the Chocolate Factory* chocolate wonderland. It was my chocolate heaven. I couldn't explain it, or justify it. I truly enjoyed those packaged pudding miracles. There was nowhere else I would rather be.

The chocolate pudding wasn't the only thing that I would enjoy in God's Waiting Room. Things got even more exciting when I started to get to know the other patients. Boy, was I in for a treat!

# new friends

Many nightmare scenarios of mental incarceration depict "sane" people being locked away in a mental hospital. They're yelling that they don't belong there, and men in white suits come and take them away. My experience wasn't quite like that. In the early days of this "incarceration," the hospital was this wondrous place to observe. All these new spirits to interact with. A little part of me was scared, but the manic part was excited, at least at first. There were so many thoughts and emotions in my head. I would get these strong emotions, and I didn't know where they came from. I would get very positive or negative feelings about different people.

The first hospital friend I remember seeing was a pregnant girl. She had strawberry blonde hair, a hint of freckles and a warm smile. She seemed so innocent and pure. There was a guy there that I thought was her boyfriend. I figured that they were together and that he abused her. I immediately knew that I was there to protect her and her unborn child. I wasn't sure how I would do this, but I kept my eye on both of them.

Then I met my roommate. It was normal to share a hospital room. I actually never formally met her; she wasn't really capable of introductions. She was a petite, well-dressed woman who looked to be about 70 or 75, the kind that would carry a different purse for different occasions. She reminded me of Estelle Getty from *The*

*Golden Girls.* She was constantly mumbling and talking, to no one. Some of the things she said would make a little sense, but most was just nonsense.

"Mother will be very upset when she finds out that the manager refused us service," she would say, and "We knew the contract was bad when we signed it." Sometimes she made eye contact, but she mostly seemed to be having conversations with someone who wasn't there. I started listening to her stories, trying to make sense of them. Maybe she was talking to someone in another dimension? To be honest, at first I was a little scared of her, but soon I began to find her quite endearing. She started to remind me of my grandmother. She would sing to herself, just like my grandmother did, as she was cleaning up her side of the room.

There was another patient in the high-security wing with me who I found very intriguing. He was a young, college-aged African-American male. A football player, he was very attractive and physically fit. He just seemed like a really nice guy. He was very polite to everyone. I think his father was a doctor at the hospital near us. His parents came to visit often. I overheard that he had anger problems. I talked with him a few times and got this really positive energy from him. I decided that he probably had some of the mania-induced powers or gifts that I had.

There was another young woman whose energy was very unsettling to me. An attractive white woman with blotchy skin, this patient felt different than the others. I thought she might be on, or trying to get off of, drugs. She looked around nervously, her hands and face twitching as she moved. I couldn't relate to her. I knew she had a lot of things that she would need to deal with.

There was a middle aged Asian-American woman who worked for the hospital. She cleaned the main area and our individual rooms each day. I also got a very good vibe from her. I was concerned about her, and felt like the hospital was taking advantage of her. She had a strong accent, and often joked with both staff and patients. We would talk a bit. She was really nice to me, and was the only staff person who would talk to me as an equal. It was refreshing not to be talked down to, or spoken to like a child. She saw *me* as a whole person, not as a mental patient.

The high-security area began to feel like the set of a sitcom. *Cheers* came to mind, but that might have been my coping mechanism. The world of sitcoms had always transported me into a safe world, a world that felt familiar. I looked at the main room of the hospital like it was a television set. Some of the patients felt like characters to me. The cleaning lady was the "neighbor" character, like Cliff Clavin. She'd stop by, make a few jokes, and then leave. The staff really helped support the illusions. Since they never saw or talked to me but continually conversed with each other, I could sit on the sofa and just watch. Just like with television, I wasn't really there in the world of the characters and story. I was the observer.

A day or two went by. I continued to eat, sleep a lot, and, of course, observe. I was a good patient. I kept my wild ideas to myself.

Then a new patient was admitted. She was my first real friend, and the first person I shared my thoughts with. I really connected with this older free spirit, new-age type of lady. She was the kind of woman who taught yoga in her earlier years, or who owned a crystal shop. She was so happy, like a breath of fresh air. Round-figured and with short hair, she wore very colorful clothes that flowed around her. She had a bubbly personality and would talk to anyone. I was very drawn to her.

At a meal she started talking about her family, and why she was in the hospital, "They just don't understand me," she sighed. "They get so mad at me when I get manic."

I could relate, not that my family got mad at me, but they didn't seem to like "manic Maggie." Then she went on to say, "They don't realize that I am being reborn, and that I'm happy."

Yes! Yes! I thought. Finally, someone who understood what I was talking about! Then she added, "I need to do this every few years to connect to this amazing energy." I was spellbound. So was having a manic episode just a way to reconnect with some sort of energy?

I decided to befriend her. And this act was the beginning of some astonishing conversations. She was, basically, teaching me about mania, and about all the marvelous secret abilities that came with it. We determined that we could both speak without speaking, or read each other's mind. We talked about our special connections with people. We shared how difficult it was to develop these skills in a world that was so against it. It was so exciting to finally have someone to talk to, to have someone who totally understood all the insights and epiphanies that I'd been thinking about for so long!

With my new friends and my writings, I felt good. I was still a little uncertain about what would happen next, but I was eager to begin. Little did I know that things were going to go downhill from there, and fast.

# the low-security area

After a few days I moved out of the high-security area and into the low-security one. I was sad to leave my friend, but I knew she would be coming to this area in a few days. In the low-security area there were a lot more public rooms, and a lot more people. The garden area on this side was bigger and was available at all times. There was even a basketball hoop. People were free to walk around the various rooms, and because of this, I began to meet a lot of new people.

My second roommate was a little more lucid. She was an older woman, about the same age as my first roommate. She was beautiful, on the inside and out. She had blonde hair, and she just seemed to glow. She lit up the room. When I think of her, I remember her in her nightgown, as she spent the majority of the day in bed, reading.

Even more than my first roommate, this person became sort of a mother figure to me. She talked to me in the same caring way that a grandmother would speak to her granddaughter. Her friendly attitude put me at ease. She gave me pointers and tricks to being in the hospital, things like how to get an extra towel. She also gave me advice. She was very at peace with the idea that she would have manic episodes every few years. It was like going to the spa, not a big deal. Her family just had to accept it. I found her inspiring. She wasn't as blatant as my other friend about her manic powers. She never really mentioned them, but I knew she had them.

I also remember meeting a young woman in one of my group meetings. She looked like a surfer girl. In San Diego there are a lot of surfer girls, and she fit the bill: long blonde hair, petite body, surfer shorts, cute tank tops, and hemp-and-shell necklace. Her personality was sweet and charming.

After a few encounters we started talking. It didn't seem like anything was wrong with her, but she explained that she had mild schizophrenia. She was married, and she actually was a real surfer. I'll never forget the way she explained her problems: "Yeah, things were going well ... then the voices started coming again." It was as if "the voices" were a familiar but unwelcome visitor who was more of a nuisance than anything to be afraid of. This was just another trip to the hospital. I admired her attitude: not really afraid but simply aware of the reality.

I also met a guy in the low-security area. Don't get any ideas. I'm still in a mental hospital, not really the greatest place to meet guys. He was in his mid-to-early twenties. He had very blonde, almost white, short hair. He was really tan, or, more precisely, sunburnt. It looked like he'd been outside for a while without any sunscreen. He talked like he was ex-military. Very polite. We hit it off at first, and started having conversations. He explained to me about how he had found God. I was like, "Me too!"

He went on. "I finally realized that I never have to worry about money. I'll always be taken care of." This is what I knew as well! Just like talking to my new friend in the high-security area, it was so nice to talk to someone who was feeling the way I was feeling. Someone who wasn't trying to tell me I was wrong, but who agreed with me. It was beyond exciting!

The excitement ended when I met my new doctor. She was a slender icy-cold woman who I guessed to be of Slavic decent due to a slight accent. She had short brown hair, a pointy noise and bluish-gray eyes. She made attempts to be nice, but somehow she came across as disingenuous and forced. I don't really remember our first conversation very well, but she must have updated me on my medications. In the hospital they had added the anti-psychotic drug Seroquel. The new med would knock me out at night, and was the reason I slept so long when I first got to the hospital. Seroquel proved to be unfortunate for the mania, but fortunate for my overall health, because it was working. The mania began to lose steam.

After several days on Seroquel and a couple of days in the low-security wing, I started questioning the whole magical bipolar thing, and with it, my transition into a new life. Again I wondered, why hadn't it happened yet? Why was I still there? When I entered the hospital I was 99% sure that I was about to cross over into a new, magical life. Once I moved to the low-security wing and away from my spiritual friend, that percentage began to go down. Each day when I awoke from taking the Seroquel the night before, the magic faded a little bit more. By the fourth or fifth day, I was starting to come to terms with the horrifying thought that oh crap ... oh no ... Maybe I am not in heaven's waiting room. Maybe I really *am* in a mental hospital.

The only thing worse than being in a mental hospital when you don't think you belong there is being in a mental hospital when you know that you do.

# coming out of psychosis — the letdown

Every day my delusions started to be less and less convincing, and the actuality of being in a mental hospital started to be more and more real. That was when I began to get scared.

As I got treatment, my belief that a new life was about to begin became more uncertain. The more treatment I got, the more my new life seemed to slip away. The more that I met with my doctors and my family, the more I realized that my vision of entering a new world might not be real.

This new, hard reality smacked me in the face when I ran into my old friend from the high-security area, the older free spirit who had related perfectly to what I'd been through. Sometimes they would let people from the high-security area come over to the low-security area for a class. They brought my friend over for a class that I was in. I walked into the room and there she was.

"Hi!" I said.

"Hello!" she smiled, with her typical bubbly personality.

"Great to see you!" I said.

She looked at me, and I could see that she was kind of confused. "What is your name?" she asked.

"It's me ... Maggie," I replied, taken aback.

"It's nice to meet you!" she said exuberantly.

She had no idea who I was! All of our talks, all of our connections, meant nothing. My heart sank.

As I stared at my supposed good friend, all of a sudden she looked different to me. She looked less wise and insightful and more weird and strange. She looked older and more worn, and the wrinkles and age spots I'd missed earlier now popped out. I looked in her eyes and saw someone who looked completely lost. She was a totally different person.

She wouldn't be the first person to change in front of my eyes.

Remember that sweet, innocent pregnant girl from the high-security area, the one who I was going to protect? A little while later, I ran into her. She was anything but sweet. Innocent was not a word I would use to describe her either. She seemed worldly in a way that bordered on, well, trashy. We started talking and I looked more closely. Not only wasn't she sweet, but she wasn't pregnant either! She was just overweight. She smiled, and I saw crooked, yellow teeth.

In addition, as the medication kicked in, I started to see that the guy I met was acting stranger and stranger. Then, after a couple of days, I began to think, this guy is really weird. He would say things at odd times. I got strange vibes from him, the kind that made me want to stay away.

I decided to not talk with him as much. Then it got uncomfortable. He gave me a note. It was a love poem. I thought, oh, of course, the one time in my life I get a love note is in a mental hospital. Yikes! Although I was still a little manic, I knew this guy was bad news. I could tell that he was annoyed that I didn't feel the same way as he did. I actually became a little afraid of him. I wondered if he might come into my room and hurt me.

I showed the note to one of the staff, and told her I was a little concerned. She, as usual, blew me off, like adults do when a child tells them about another kid hurting her feelings. I just did my best to keep my distance, and, thankfully, the issue fizzled.

The staff continued to treat us like we were little children. Their words, body language, and actions underscored the perception that they were normal and we were the mental patients. They made me feel like I was, well, crazy. I could sense that they looked down on me, and they certainly didn't take any pains to conceal it.

This judgment came out in one of the activities I attended. It was some sort of goal-setting activity, and the teacher was using a kind of art therapy. A small group of us, about five people, sat at a spacious table in one of the side rooms. There was a nice, big window that bathed the room in light. Bookshelves lined the walls, and there were bins filled with art supplies. The facilitator was a warm and friendly woman in her early thirties. She had shoulder-length, curly blonde hair. I knew her type. She had her "I'm *helping* people!" attitude on. I could tell that she felt good about herself, like she was giving-back-to-the-world, having to work with all us crazies, how noble of her. If I were not in the hospital she would have talked to me with a completely different tone. She would have talked to me as an equal, instead of as if I were in pre-school.

"Okay everybody!" she said, in her teacher-friendly voice. "Today we're going to depict our goals by making pictures!" She passed out blank sheets of paper to each of us, and deposited a pile of colored pencils on the table. She went on to explain, "When you draw a picture of where you want to be, it helps you see what your future could look like!"

Duh, I thought. I already knew that if you put what was in your head onto the paper in the form of a picture, it helped bring this image into reality. I realized this, by the way, *when* I was manic. To an extent, I still believe this today. If you focus on things you want to happen, they are more likely to do so.

Then she said, "Now, on this piece of paper I want you to draw a picture of where you will be in six months."

I thought for a minute and knew exactly what to draw. I knew I was going to be a professional stand-up comic. So I drew what represented stand-up comedy in my mind. I drew a stage with a brick wall background. A brick wall background is very common for comedy clubs. Then I drew a microphone and shaft of light on the stage that came from a spotlight. Drawing people isn't one of my fortes, so I just left it like that.

The counselor-facilitator came over to me and said, "Wow, how nice. I love your drawing!"

I may have still been partially manic, but I knew condescension when I heard it.

"What does it mean?"

"This is a comedy club stage," I responded, "because I'm going to be a stand-up comedian."

She tried to hide a look that went from shock to disbelief, and then to a kind of pity.

"Well, isn't that great!" she said. "Good for you!" The fact that she said the same thing to just about everyone in the room clued me in that she just might be patronizing me. It made me start to doubt myself even more.

The next day I started to observe the other patients from a different point of view. My new roommate didn't look near as bright and angelic. All of a sudden I could see that she was actually quite elderly and frail. None of the patients seemed special any more. Oh, man I thought, these people aren't magical beings. They are f-ing crazy!

At that point, the percentage of my belief that I was a magical being continued to dramatically decrease every day. Being in a mental hospital: it's like the whole world was telling me that my beliefs are wrong. They're so wrong, in fact, that they have to keep me away from society. Even worse is that, after a while, I started to believe them. Maybe they're right. Maybe I am sick. Maybe I am defective. I can't even begin to tell you how disappointing it is to realize that you might not be magical, you might just be crazy.

I remember sitting in the garden and staring at the fence, the fence with the black metal bars that separated me from the outside world. I now realized that those bars in the fence were meant not to protect me from the world, but to protect the world from me. The world didn't want me. I sat there and cried and cried and cried. I cried because the whole situation was awful. More important, I knew it was only going to get worse.

# the darkness of mania

I sat there in the garden wondering, how did I get here? How did I let this happen? I hadn't completely given up on the existence of a new life for me. But the reality of where I had ended up was becoming apparent. Just a month earlier I was living a normal life. I was on my way to a lucrative and successful career. I had everything going for me. Now I was in a mental hospital with a bunch of crazies. Mania had come into my life like a tornado, destroying everything that I cared about. I was starting to see just how powerful mania, bipolar disorder, and mental illness could truly be, and more important, how powerless I was to stop it.

Trying to explain mania is like trying to explain a dream. Just like a dream, mania can go from breathtakingly wonderful to terrifying in an instant. Although you are experiencing some extraordinary and magical moments, you're also going through some of the most gut-wrenching pain that you've ever felt. You have absolutely no control over the emotions, good or bad.

When I look back on this third manic episode, my memories are almost unbelievable to me. At the beginning of the episode, I felt as if I existed in reality, but with a surreal layer on top of it. At first the surreal layer was light and ephemeral, but as I got more and more consumed by the illness, the layer got thicker and thicker, until I could barely see the reality anymore. At first I tried to ignore the surreal layer, but as it grew and swelled, it became so real that I could no longer distinguish it from the reality around me.

This layer found its way into my life. It came first as enlightenment: beauty was more beautiful, nature was more wondrous, and I was the master of my own wonderful destiny. Eventually I started to believe the good feelings, because these were the ones that felt the most real, these were the ones that felt right. I was so consumed by the phenomenal possibilities of life that I couldn't function in reality.

I felt this strong connection to something amazing, to a force, or to a presence, whether defined as God or any other higher power. I felt a connection that was so rich and so mind-numbingly wonderful that I let go of my own reality so that I could continue to feel it. To make matters worse, it felt like everyone in my life that I cared about was trying to stop me. Why would they do this? Why would they stop me from this joy? I had no answer to this, and so I pulled away from my family and friends. I said awful things to them, because they did not understand. It seemed like they weren't even trying to understand me. They were, in fact, my old life.

Once I started getting treatment in the hospital, I slowly realized that those excited, blissful feelings, that surreal layer, might not be real. I started doubting myself. I was no longer confident, I was afraid. The dream-psychosis began to turn into a nightmare. The awesome beauty of the enlightenment started to slip away, and was replaced by uncertainty, fear and failure. When manic, or coming down from mania, you can't stop the terrible, terrible, terrible, terrible and painful, painful, painful emotions. Or the images and thoughts that flood your mind. I remember when I was sixteen years old and coming out of mania, I had an apocalyptic vision: a volcano erupted, spewing lava and fire that flowed in gushing streams around me. It was a nightmare, except I was awake.

Now, as an adult, the pain of mania found clever ways to sneak into my reality. Sometimes in the hospital and even afterwards,

I'd be ambushed by an overwhelming feeling of darkness, along with a scared, foreboding ache, and have no idea why. When I was in the proximity of certain people, I would feel terrible, as if I were absorbing all of their negative energy. At times it felt as if I were possessed by a dark spirit that dropped me to the depths of anguish. Perhaps I needed a priest to come and do on exorcism on me.

When you're blinded by mania, it becomes really hard to distinguish what's real. In the beginning, the mania convinced me that my life as I knew it was not real compared to the new life or dimension I would be going to. Life as I knew it had no substance, nothing about it was as I had perceived it. My family wasn't real. Friends weren't real. Sights and sounds weren't real. Objects weren't even real. Now in the hospital I didn't know what was real, or more important, who I was. I had no solid ground to stand on.

The fear that gripped me was bad enough. The way I was treated didn't help either. Imagine thinking that you have found the key to the universe, and no one believes you. Not only do they not believe you, they lock you up until you don't believe it yourself anymore. When I was really manic, I didn't care that I was in a mental hospital, but as I came out of it, being there felt awful. I was filled with shame and embarrassment

Moreover, I was so afraid. I didn't know what dimension I was in. I didn't complete my transition. I was no longer in God's Waiting Room. I sure wasn't in heaven. So where was I? I had *no* idea of how to proceed in the world.

Sitting in that garden, I remember wanting to make sure that I didn't forget what I was experiencing. I needed something to compare it to, so that I could help others understand. I remember telling myself that the pain was so bad that I would rather have been a hostage in a foreign prison, beaten every day, than have an episode and be put in a mental hospital. If I were a prisoner, as horrific as that would be, there would, at least, be the possibility of release and freedom. Being in a mental hospital in the throes of mania was different, because I knew I would never escape my own mind, nor the torture it put me through.

I would have to go through this pain alone. I thought I had an intimate and awesome connection to God, but as I got treatment, the connection started to fade. Even more devastating, my relationship with my family and friends was damaged. I couldn't just go back to the way it had been. I was stuck picking up the pieces that the mania left behind. I not only felt disconnected to God, but to my entire life. I felt totally and completely alone.

I compare the experience of coming down from mania to that of someone who is on a boat in a perfect storm. At first the waves are breathtaking, mesmerizing, thirty stories high. You're in awe of this spectacular ocean and its power. The waves are awesome! Coasting up and down the waves is exhilarating, as the power picks you up and propels you forward, faster than you have ever gone in your life.

Then the waves shift, and suddenly they're coming right at you! It is terrifying. You get thrown from the boat, and you're in the ocean. Alone. You see your family, the people you love most. They're still on the boat, which is now *sinking!* Until you can no longer see them. You are left there, floating in an endless ocean, alone. Everything that you ever cared about is gone. You don't know if you will ever get it back.

When engulfed in the darkness, you think the sense of hopelessness will last forever. The loneliness is excruciating. Despite all the amazing feelings that I experienced in the beginning of mania, feelings of ecstasy and feelings of enlightenment, this is where I ended up, alone and caged in a mental hospital. I experienced heaven, but to return to reality I would have to go through hell.

# adjusting to treatment

After I had been in the hospital for almost a week, I knew that I had to return to reality—but it would prove to be a very slow trip back. It wasn't just like, oh okay, now I'm not crazy anymore! You can't just snap out of it. Fortunately, the magical part of the mania didn't go away completely. If it had, the devastating depression that hit when I realized my life had been shattered would have probably killed me. Part of me still believed that it was possible that I had become enlightened, and part of me was beginning to see that my life was a mess. I was coming to terms with the reality of the hospitalization, but still a little hopeful that something amazing might still happen.

The hospital staff's continual fake congeniality began to really bother me. I felt just like another body. It was obvious that we weren't on the same level as them. They told us the rules and watched us: again, the equivalent of really expensive babysitting. Like automatons, they continued to approach us every few hours, pencil in hand.

"Have you heard any voices?

"No."

"Have you had any delusions?"

"No."

You could have been in the middle of an intense discussion with Queen Elizabeth, or Mahatma Gandhi, or Captain Kirk, and they'd still ask you the same questions and walk away. Unless we were swinging from the chandelier or bludgeoning another patient, what we did or thought didn't matter. If you want to feel like you're worthless, stay in a mental hospital for a few days. Then you'll know you don't matter.

One of my last days in the hospital, I was in the television room. Two staff members were there, too, watching *American Idol.* Most of the patients left the room, leaving just the two ladies and me. We watched the *American Idol* episode, and for a while I forgot that I was the patient and they were the staff. I made a comment about the show in a way that I would speak with my friends. A comment that a "normal" person would make. I will never forget their reaction. Both of them looked at me, and paused. It was as if they were thinking, "Um … why are you talking to us? In case you didn't notice, we're not friends or anything. And it's not like you'd have any valid opinions." They gave me a brief look up and down, and then turned back to each other and started their own conversation.

My psychiatrist was also annoying me. As I mentioned, I met her on the first or second day I arrived, but I was pretty out of it so I don't remember our conversation. Now that I was a little more lucid I remember talking with her.

"Hello Maah-ga-ret," she said, with a slight accent. "You look much better." I smiled back at her. Then she went on, "I don't know if you remember but you vere very argumentative ven you arrived." I thought back but couldn't remember. "Oh, I am sorry. I wasn't thinking clearly." She nodded, "Yes, you disagreed with my plan to lower your Vellbutrin." She said it almost with a little laugh. As if to say, how absurd it would be for *me* to argue with *her.* Feeling like it was established who was making the decisions, she glanced at my file and then looked up at me and said, without emotion, "So, ve did lower your Vellbutrin by half, to help reduce the mania." Not expecting any reaction, she lowered her gaze and looked at my file again.

"I don't think that's a good idea," I said. "I think we should keep the same dose."

She looked up at me, startled. She seemed surprised, and a little offended, that I'd questioned her, again. "I am sorry, vot did you say?"

"I should stay on this dose," I replied. "I tried to go off it once, a few years ago, and it was a disaster."

She tried to hide her irritation. Then she repeated, "It is important dat you do not get manic again, so we are cutting your Vellbutrin. Dis will be best for you. Dere is no more to discuss."

That was that. She reminded me of a villain in a James Bond movie, or even of the iconic Natasha from the Rocky and Bullwinkle cartoons. She heard nothing that I said, and had learned nothing from my medical history. I had been on Lithium and Wellbutrin for ten years. I knew exactly how they affected me. I don't want to brag, but this was not my first rodeo. At the age of sixteen, I became an expert in taking potent medications.

I guess I should have been thankful that my doctor was at least telling me what I was about to take. When I was in the hospital at age sixteen, it was a totally different experience. The staff just gave us pills and told us to swallow them. It was 1994, so treatment wasn't as good as it is today. I was so young that I just did what I was told to do. There would be an announcement for everyone to check in with the nurse, and all the teenage patients would line up at the window of the nurses' station. I would tell them my name and they would give me a cup full of different-colored pills. The first time I got the cup I must have stared at it for a second or two, because the nurse said, "Honey, don't think about it too much. Just swallow them all at once. It'll be easier that way."

Now, at the age of twenty-six and in my third hospitalization, after a decade of taking medication every single day, I had a good understanding of how the medication affected me. I felt I knew what I needed better than this doctor did, the doctor who had only known me for a few days. I wanted to talk back to the doctor and disagree.

Show my rebellious cool side. Maybe rant like Angelina Jolie in *Girl Interrupted*. She did win an Academy Award for that role.

However, if I wanted to get out of there, I needed to play nice. I decided to placate "Dr. Natasha" and accept her changes. At that point I didn't have much choice. If I wanted to get released, I would have to go along with the program. This wasn't Hollywood. So I did the only thing that I could do, just smile and nod.

# getting out of the hospital

My playing nice with the doctor worked out for the best. After a little over a week of being in the hospital, I was deemed ready to be released. I was a lot better than when I first got there, but I definitely was not back to normal. I wasn't in full-blown mania or psychosis, but I was still slightly manic, with a very small hint of psychosis. Inside I was still confused. I didn't think I was in God's Waiting Room or about to go to heaven or to a new dimension. But I couldn't let go of all of those manic feelings. I still held the faint possibility that my life would change into something spectacular, that I would be starting a new life with new abilities or encountering unexpected success. I didn't know how it would happen, but I still felt that it might.

Despite the lingering mania and psychosis, I may have appeared perfectly normal to the doctors because I knew how to hide my feelings. I knew how to behave and act. That is what's so interesting about mental illness. People can look very "normal," but you have no idea of what's actually going through their heads. Again I was playing the role of Maggie Newcomb. I would say things that I knew would pass, safe thoughts and topics. I knew not to mention any of my manic ideals or dreams.

Luckily, even though I was released from the hospital, Dr. Natasha was aware that it would take many, many months before I would be able to return to my normal life. I had been through a very serious trauma and the worst thing to do would be to put me back into the life that had created this shattering episode. It is very common for people to relapse back into mania and psychosis if they try to go back to their lives too soon. I had experienced that when I was sixteen, and consequently my relapse was worse than my first hospitalization.

Doctor Natasha gave me prescriptions for my medications that would last for a few months. I could see her in outpatient sessions temporarily in San Diego, but when I got back to Oakland, I would need to find a new psychiatrist. I could also see my therapist for cognitive therapy. My treatment plan was to keep taking my regular medications of Lithium and Wellbutrin as well as Seroquel and Ambien at night to combat the mania. I needed to relax and not get stressed, so that my mind would heal.

This meant that I couldn't go back to my job for quite some time. My doctor put me on disability for five months. Normal Maggie would have been devastated and embarrassed to be on disability. This went against everything that I had believed in and strived for. However, in my current condition, I didn't care. In fact, I didn't know if I would ever be able to work again. Despite my lingering manic fantasies, at that point I was still very weak emotionally. I was still so confused. The hard-working spirit that used to define me was broken.

After I was released from the hospital, I went to stay with my parents. We agreed that I would stay there until I was well enough to go back to Oakland. When I arrived back at my parents' house, the awful memories of the prior week greeted me. I felt like I was returning to the battlefield after a war. Ghosts of the past manic, angry and upset Maggie still hovered in the air. I put my stuff into my old childhood room and sat on the bed. I looked at all the happy pictures on the wall of my family and me. Who was that girl? Was that me? I sighed and thought to myself, "Now what?" In the background I heard the phone ring. It was one of my roommates calling from Oakland. My mom came into the room with the phone and I shook my head. I didn't want to talk to anybody.

There's something you must understand: coming home from the mental hospital is like coming back to a job that you quit. Not the kind of quitting where you give two weeks and they throw you a going-away party. The kind where you tell your boss that he or she is a complete idiot and a terrible manager. As you leave with your stuff, you also yell at your coworkers, "You all can go f— yourselves! I am never coming back here again!" Then somehow you get your job back, and you have to return to the office. All your coworkers are staring at you as you slowly put your stuff back in your cubicle, feeling embarrassed and ashamed.

Although I never told my friends and family to f— off, I wasn't exactly sad to leave them. When I was manic I was restless to start a new life without them. And now I was back. The best way to describe my experience with my family and friends in the several months after my hospitalization is with the office analogy above—it was awwwk-ward. Although I was no longer in full-on psychosis, I wasn't completely back to normal either. I was about sixty percent normal, and part of me still dreamed of the wonderful times I'd had when I was manic. There were still flickers of hope. I held onto the belief that, just maybe, I wasn't crazy. Part of me secretly believed the possibility that I could have a miraculous transition into my new life. Therefore, I wasn't thrilled to see my family and friends, for they were a reminder that these dreams of mine weren't real.

Mania felt like an ex-boyfriend. We'd done our thing and now part of me knew it needed to be over. I had to move on. Just like getting over a relationship, you try to move on, but a part of you still reminisces about the good times. I knew that my family and friends wanted it to be over as well. They hated my mania. In some ways I didn't blame them. They couldn't experience the excitement, confidence and joy that I was feeling. They had slowly lost the person that they had known and loved.

Although I was still recovering, I had to deal with something difficult that I had avoided: my job. Two weeks had passed since I told my boss that I needed time off. They were expecting me back at work. However, I was now on disability and I couldn't work. I needed to inform the company of this. It felt like a lifetime ago that I had left that message with my boss.

I was still very, very angry with my supervisor, and I blamed her for my episode. So I called human resources instead. I told the HR staffer that I had had a breakdown and was on disability for a few months. I remember crying on the phone with her. I was so ashamed. This was a company that I had dreamed of being with for a long time. I had wanted to be CEO one day. Now I was calling to tell them that I'd just gotten out of a mental hospital. I was devastated.

Several hours later my supervisor called back. She left a message, telling me that I was "separated from the company." (FYI: It is illegal to fire an employee after he or she goes on disability. Thank God!) She didn't say anything else. No thank you for your service, or I hope you feel better. Just, that I was basically fired. However, HR must have filled her in on the law. She called back later and retracted her earlier statement; I wasn't separated from the company.

I spent the next few weeks with my parents trying to get back to that "normal" that everyone wanted. I went on long walks. I journaled. I tried doing art projects with my mom. I watched a lot of television alone and with my dad. My parents and I would have dinner every night together. I mostly just puttered around our house for several weeks. When no one was looking, I sat in our kitchen and just stared at the backyard for hours.

However, the mania still lingered. Then something strange happened at that time that I still can't explain to this day. Although

I felt alienated from my family and close friends, I felt oddly connected to those who had died. Weird, right? I felt the presence of my grandmother, who had died several years earlier. She was my mother's mother. I just felt that she was with me. My grandmother was a beautiful woman, one of those too-rare individuals, a woman with a sparkle in her eye. She wore her hair pulled back, shiny, black hair, flecked with gray, and she always wore turquoise. A very loving grandma, who, when I was age four through twelve, would take me shopping and teach me about gardening and art. I can't explain it, I just felt her warmth around me, and when I did, I knew she was trying to help me. I had never felt her presence like this before. It was just another indication that maybe the mania was still there.

I had hoped the mania would go away faster. I knew that I was still not myself because in addition to thinking my grandma was communicating with me, I did several strange things that I'm still embarrassed about. I still had really strong feelings for that comedian friend who I thought that I had fallen in love with. I still held out hope that maybe we could be together, but I kept that to myself. I wasn't sure if he felt the same. Like all my friends, he was concerned about me. After I got out of the hospital we chatted on the phone a few times. I always felt good after I spoke with him. I think we even wrote each other letters. Still not romantic, just friends.

He told me that he planned to come down to San Diego to visit me soon. I was convinced that once he saw me he would maybe fall in love with me and see how we were meant to be together. I couldn't wait to see him. I wanted our reunion to be perfect! I would have visions that we had been together for multiple lifetimes and now we were finally going to be together forever.

Now this is where it gets weird, I mean really weird. If this was a funky disco song someone in the background would be yelling "Saaay Whaaaat?" Okay, I am going to admit a dirty secret. I believed that his mother, who had died several years earlier, was trying to tell me that we were supposed to be together. I didn't hear her voice, I just felt like she needed me to save him. She knew that, only together, would he reach his true potential. How did she tell me this? I just felt it. I can't explain it. My feelings for him were already there and this push from his mom meant that I actually had to be the instigator.

When he arrived, I acted normal. I knew I had to approach him when we were in some sort of romantic setting. I believe that we were walking on the beach when I told him that I wanted to *be* with him. I told him that I had romantic feelings for him and we were meant to be together. Like a good friend, he was flattered but he didn't feel the same way. Now, if I was normal I would have never done this in the first place. At first I accepted his refusal and wanted to move on. But, I was getting this nagging push from his mom. She seemed to be telling me not to give up.

So, later when we sat on the beach, I did what any crazy person that was getting signs from his dead mom would do, I tried to kiss him. He pushed me away—and I tried again. He pushed me away again. At this point he started getting angry. We got up and walked back to the car. I felt he had to know. This whole thing was not my idea. It was his mom wanting me to do this. So, I told him about why I was doing it. It was his mom pressuring me. Yeah, that didn't go over too well. He became very angry at me (with good reason). He yelled at me, "You are bringing up my Mom!?" then went on, "You are really starting to offend me!" I finally took the hint and shut up.

We drove back to my parents' house in silence. That little incident worried him, so he told my parents about it. Everyone thought I was doing so well up until that point. I was able to hide these delusions from everyone. I was actually just a few days away from going back to Oakland. He told my parents that I was still manic, and that he felt I needed more time before I went back to Northern California. He was right to tell them that, but, at the time, I didn't like it at all. I wanted to get back to Oakland. I was furious at him! The last day he was there I barely spoke to him. I wanted nothing to do with him. He went back to Oakland.

I just want to add here, that after the mania ended, I no longer heard from my friend's mom. That is what we call a delusion or distorted thinking. I do believe that our loved ones that have died are still with us. I think it's possible they give us little signs or feeling of encouragement. However, I do not believe that they ask us to do things. I can believe that maybe my grandma was with me to perhaps comfort me, but that is it.

After my comedian friend left, it had been more than a month since my release date from the hospital, and I was ready for a change. I loved my parents, but I badly wanted to go back to my old life. There was nothing for me down in San Diego. However, my parents still felt that I needed to stay with them. They were adamant about it. We even argued. I told them that I would go back anyway, but my mom said that they wouldn't let me use their car. I was stuck. So, I did something I'd never actually done before: I ran away from home. That's right, at twenty-six, I ran away from home.

# going rogue

This wasn't the first time I attempted to run away. In fact, in 6th grade I tried to run away because I was infuriated with my parents, probably for some silly reason. I was going to show *them*. I packed a bag for myself. I added dog food for my dog Wilson who would, of course, be accompanying me on the journey. Just the two of us against the world. I told my Dad in a very threatening 6th-grader tone, "I am running away!" After having heard this several times before, my Dad knew how to react.

With equal amounts of sarcasm and belittling he responded, "Okay! Let me know if you need help packing."

I was furious! How dare he? I grabbed Wilson's leash and put it on him. I yelled, one more time, "I mean it! Here we go!" I slowly walked to our backyard, which had a gate that led to a main road. I got to the gate and opened it. Wilson and I walked out. We looked at the main road, which had traffic of all sorts whizzing by. I was filled with fear. Then I looked back at the house. There was my dad in the patio. He waved.

"Margie, why don't we go inside and talk about this?" All of a sudden that seemed like a better idea than escaping down this busy road. I closed the gate and my dad came out and gave me a hug. That was the end of my journey in 6th grade.

Well, that was then and this is now. Despite all my failed attempts, this time at age 26, I was going to do it. I was going to run away and I was going to be successful.

I walked to the nearest Starbucks and called a cab. Luckily I had a credit card—and the manic principles were still with me. This meant that I didn't have any problem spending $75 on a cab ride to the airport. Money was still just energy. I knew that whatever I spent would always come back to me. I could buy whatever I needed.

I had gone rogue. At the airport I decided that I would rather drive than fly, so I rented a car for the trip up north. I found the biggest, best and most expensive SUV I could find. The most important thing was that I felt good. This behavior was not like me. In my normal state I would never have gotten an SUV. So impractical, and such bad gas mileage.

I was going to drive up the coast back to my house, up Highway 101 in my SUV rental car. Although I knew I was fine, my family and friends at the time were worried sick. They didn't know where I was going. They were the ones who were trying to hold me back.

I got on the road in my luxury SUV, stopping for food and gas whenever I wanted to. It felt good to be alone, to be in control. I blared the music and sang along as I drove next to the glistening Pacific Ocean. After about five hours I decided to stop in Shell Beach near San Luis Obispo. I chose to stay at a very nice hotel, charging everything on my dwindling credit card. I chose that hotel because several years earlier I had stayed there with Grandma, and it made me feel good to be there again.

The hotel was on the cliff, overlooking the Pacific Ocean. This inn was an unusual mix of the old and new, a sort of Wuthering-Heights-meets-California-resort type of feeling. I went to a fancy restaurant that was near the hotel and that overlooked the ocean. I bought whatever I wanted, appetizers, beer, and one of the most expensive entrees. I sat there alone in that beautiful place, gazing at the water of the Pacific Ocean as it broke against the shore. A small part of me thought, "What are you *doing?*" I ignored the thought and went back to my fresh salmon with garlic mashed potatoes and creamed spinach. Of course, when the bill came, the high price didn't bother me, and I tipped generously.

I was enjoying the adventure, but I was a little scared. I still didn't know who I was. Part of me felt like I needed to be there, to get away. I deserved to be happy. The other part felt like I was on the run, a misunderstood fugitive.

I felt guilty, so I called my parents and told them I was safe. I told them that I was fine and that I would be in Oakland the next day. I got off the phone as quickly as I could. I didn't need their negative energy. I turned on the television in the hotel room, and was immediately relieved when *Seinfeld* appeared on the screen. Hearing George Costanza yell at Kramer brought me home and helped me relax. It was a feeling I could understand. Sitcoms could always take me away from the pain or fear of my life. They shut everything out.

The next day I woke up in the sunlit hotel room. I packed up my stuff. Then I saw my journal on the bed. The journal that I had been writing in after I got out of the hospital. It represented a lot of pain, and a helpless Maggie. I decided to throw it in the garbage. I didn't need that bad energy on this trip. I also stole the Bible from the hotel drawer. I figured Jesus would want to come with me on my adventure. I got back in the SUV and drove about 5 hours back to Oakland.

When I arrived, my roommates were there. My parents had called to let them know I was coming, and they'd been extremely worried. They were a little upset with me, but ultimately glad to see that I was okay.

I was back on my home turf, but things were still very awkward for me. I have the most loving, caring and supportive friends. However, I didn't want to see them. They were the ex-coworkers that I had told to f— off in my mind. They were constant reminders to me that I was neither special nor enlightened. I was just sick.

The day I got home, the parents of one of my roommates were visiting. They asked if they could take us to a restaurant. So we all went to dinner, as if nothing had ever happened. Our table buzzed with small talk. I tried my best to play along, but inside I was troubled, and confused. We were in a small, crowded Italian restaurant near our house, an establishment and an evening that I would have normally loved. But this night I just sat there and looked around. The room was filled with people who were eating, talking, and laughing, people who were living their lives. I had never felt so alone.

I'm sure it was probably awkward for my friends as well. I'm pretty sure I was still acting a little strange. The real Maggie wouldn't return for several more months. For the next several weeks I tried to remember who I was. And I tried to channel that person, to call her back into my life.

I was trying to get better, but the progress was slow. For a very long time, I could not relate to my closest friends. How could I? They hadn't been where I'd been. They wanted to help me, and they did help me, and I am so grateful that they did. They wanted "me" back.

The problem was, I didn't know who "me" was. Was I Maggie the enlightened being, or Maggie the mental patient? At that point I didn't want to be either.

# was everything lost?

After returning to Oakland, things did not get any easier for me. As I struggled to get back to normal, the reality and the repercussions of being in a mental hospital were just starting to come to the surface. After being hospitalized, you can't just go back to your life as if nothing ever happened. Imagine telling your boss, "Oh yeah, just got back from the psych ward, and I can't wait to start working with our clients again!" That doesn't happen. Being in a mental hospital is like declaring bankruptcy on your reputation. It's as if your regular clothes have disappeared, and now you have a big red C (for crazy) on your chest. (My sophomore English teacher would be very impressed with that reference.)

With my return to Oakland, I felt naked and vulnerable to the world. Before my third episode, only a few very close friends and family knew about my two hospitalizations ten years earlier. Now everyone knew! My co-workers, all my relatives, all my friends, all my parents' friends, my comedian friends. I was so embarrassed. I had been outed. And now that I had, no one could figure out what to do with me. Nobody knew how to treat me or how to react. Nobody would even talk about this huge experience we'd all just had. I could tell that they had no idea what to say. It was extremely uncomfortable. It wasn't just an elephant in the room, it was a big, woolly mammoth, and it followed me everywhere.

More important, I felt like I had lost everything that I'd worked so hard for in the last ten years. All my accomplishments seemed to mean nothing. All my hard work to show the world that I wasn't "crazy" now seemed pointless. All that I had accomplished in the past ten years was going to be overshadowed by this new third episode and hospitalization. The title of "mental patient" eclipsed every other title I'd ever earned: college graduate, employee, coach, athlete, friend, teammate, and survivor.

Those few weeks are sort of fuzzy. I know that I stayed home while my roommates went to work. I journaled, and I went on walks. I still wasn't all there, so I continued to play the role of "Maggie Newcomb." I was an imposter in my own life and home. The glistening Lake Merritt, once vibrant and beautiful to me, was now hazy and dull.

I tried to cheer myself up. In an attempt to recreate some of the magic that I'd felt in the hospital, I went to the store and bought whatever foods felt good to me. My roommates were confused when they opened the refrigerator door to see rows of pudding cups and other highly processed comfort foods. But when I ate the chocolate pudding cups, they tasted like chemicals. The heavenly magic was gone.

I still didn't feel close with my roommates. Their lives seemed so foreign to me. The once-fun dinner parties now felt obligatory. I sat through the dinner, and smiled and nodded. (I had gotten very good at that.) Then I would go to my room. I could hear them laughing and shouting as they drank and socialized. I wanted to do that too, but I couldn't.

Nothing felt normal to me. I recall thinking: I just want to remember what Friday feels like. Every day now felt the same. You know that feeling when you know it's Friday and the weekend is coming? You just feel good. Every day has a feeling, right? Even Sunday. That's the day that you're kind of bummed that you have to go back to work. I longed for those simple feelings to come back, even the bad ones. I had taken all of them, everything, for granted. Sanity was no longer a given. I had to find it.

Then there were my finances. Before my third episode I was debt-free. I wasn't rolling in dough, but I was financially independent. After I got back from the hospital, I faced a truckload of financial issues. Not only had I been using my credit card in ways that I wouldn't have normally done, but my disability payments were my only income. I started to incur a mounting debt. At one point, the balance in my bank account was negative nine cents. This was especially troublesome considering that, according to my doctors, it would be a long time until I would be able to work again, at least several months. The way that I felt in my slow recovery, I still wasn't sure if I would *ever* be able to work again.

I was embarrassed to be on disability, but it was my only option. My parents were very clear that I could stay with them, but that they wouldn't give me money. It was their version of tough love, and since my dad was no longer working, they didn't have the money to give me anyway. There wasn't anyone to bail me out. I had to come back on my own. Looking back, this was probably the best thing that my parents could have done for me.

Despite all that was going on, at least I still had my comedy dream. That was still alive. My doctors and my family had asked me not to do comedy for several months. They didn't think that I was ready, and were concerned that the pressure of performance might lead to another manic episode. I didn't agree. I needed to do it. So, a couple months after the hospitalization, I embarked upon a mini-comedy revolt. I wrote a set all about bipolar disorder, and about my experiences in the hospital. Then, like a teenager en route to a late-night beer blast, I snuck out of the house. The show was at a comedy club in San Francisco, and was presented by the San Francisco Comedy College. I hadn't done a big show since I'd been hospitalized. I was sure I had a brilliant set ready to go.

Oh boy, was I wrong. I got on stage and the ugliness began. The jokes I wrote were pretty good, but it was too soon. I was speaking way, way too fast. My timing was off. The jokes about bipolar disorder came off sad instead of funny, and I could tell that they made the audience feel really uncomfortable. That magical comedy energy I'd had when I performed during my slightly manic run-up to my last episode was not there. Many of my jokes fell flat. Man, it hurt badly. I realized that I needed more time to recover. I wasn't ready to be joking about what I'd just been through. It would be several more weeks before I was ready to get back on stage.

It seemed like everything was taking longer than I'd planned. I wasn't recovering nearly as fast as I thought I should. As spring slowly turned to summer, I had to make the heart-wrenching decision to miss my brother's wedding in France. I didn't miss the irony of it all: one of the reasons I'd worked so hard at my job at the media research company was so that I could get time off to go to my brother's wedding. The insane work hours I'd endured had helped drive me into mania, and now I would miss the wedding. I needed more time to recover. I was hospitalized in April, and my brother's wedding was in July. I knew I wouldn't be able to handle it. The time change, the traveling. I wasn't ready. I could barely function with a life of doing nothing. I didn't want to go there and lose it and then ruin his wedding. It seemed much safer for me to stay at home.

It was the right thing to do, but to this day it still hurts that I missed it. My brother is very special to me, and missing his wedding was a profound disappointment. Despite my manic dreams of getting away from my family, I truly love them. Missing this major event in my family's life was painful. I had already paid for my ticket to France. The plans were already made. I just couldn't step into them.

My family was very sad that I wasn't coming, but they understood. However, they were worried about going to France for several weeks and leaving me alone. My mom, especially, didn't want to leave me, but she couldn't miss her only son's wedding. By that time, it had been several months since the hospitalization, and I was finally able to take care of myself. It wasn't ideal for me to be alone but it was okay. I also had relatives and close friends in town who could help.

I needed to focus on my recovery so that I didn't have a relapse, like I'd had at the age of sixteen. However, it was hard to focus on a recovery when there was so much to bring me down.

# lurking depression

In the summer of 2004, I felt like I had a lot to be depressed about. I was on disability, I was incurring financial debt, I couldn't relate to my friends, I wasn't able to do stand-up and, to top it off, my whole family was in France having fun at my brother's wedding.

Then, later in the summer, things got even worse. The lease at our house in Oakland was about to be up in September, and I knew that my disability income would not be enough for me to pay rent somewhere else. I needed to figure out what I was going to do. My sister convinced me to move in with her and her husband in the fall. They were moving to Woodland, California so that her husband could go to the University of California, Davis for his MBA. I felt awful about having to encroach upon their lives, but I had no choice.

Losing my ability to support myself really affected me. On top of the confusion and isolation I was already feeling, not to mention the shame, guilt, and loss of identity, now I also felt like a real failure. Any motivation I had to get better started to slip away. I stopped trying to cheer myself up. I didn't care about anything anymore. Sometimes I would stay in bed all day. Or else I'd spend the whole day watching television. The big part of my day was walking out to the mailbox to see if my disability check had come in.

For a few days I watched *The Surreal Life* marathon on VH1, a reality show about "famous" people living in a house together. That season it starred Flavor Flav and Brigitte Nielsen, the rapper and the 80s action star who was Sylvester Stallone's ex-girlfriend. They had a strange romance. One minute they are screaming at each other, the next minute they are making out. I would go to bed thinking about Brigitte Nielsen and wake up thinking about Brigitte Nielsen. I thought to myself, these people are on television and I'm the crazy one?

I desperately wanted to avoid falling into depression, something that is incredibly common after a manic episode. Depression is awful. When you're in depression, you don't think you will ever come out of it. You are blinded by feelings of hopelessness, and there are absolutely no positive outcomes in sight.

It is sometimes a bit frustrating when you decide to tell someone about your depression, and he or she responds, "I know what you mean. I have my ups and downs every day too." A lot of people have down periods or get temporarily depressed, but that isn't necessarily clinical depression. Being in a depressed state is painful, but it doesn't cut as deeply or last as long as clinical depression. If someone is temporarily depressed, there is a reason for it. It's normal, and hopefully when the circumstances change, the depressive state goes away. Clinical depression is a dark cloud that comes over you, and one that often needs no reason for its arrival. You can't find a way out of its blackness.

Like mania, the depths of depression can be difficult to put into words. So I will borrow some from something I read online. A friend showed me this description of depression not long after the actor Lee Thompson Young committed suicide in August of 2013. Although it was posted on a site in response to someone who'd called the young actor a coward for deserting his family and friends, the description has been around since 2010.

*Depression is humiliating. It turns intelligent, kind people into zombies who can't wash a dish or change their socks. It affects the ability to think clearly, to feel anything, to ascribe value to your children, your lifelong passions, your relative good fortune. It scoops out your normal healthy ability to cope with bad days and bad news, and replaces it with an unrecognizable sludge that finds no pleasure, no delight, no point in anything outside of bed. You alienate your friends because you can't comport yourself socially, you risk your job because you can't concentrate, and you live in moderate squalor because you have no energy to stand up, let alone take out the garbage. You become pathetic and you know it. And you have no capacity to stop the downward plunge. You have no perspective, no emotional reserves, no faith that it will get better. So you feel guilty and ashamed of your inability to deal with life like a regular human, which exacerbates the depression and the isolation. If you've never been depressed, thank your lucky stars and back off the folks who take a pill so they can make eye contact with the grocery store cashier. No one on earth would choose the nightmare of depression over an averagely turbulent normal life. [Depression] is not an incapacity to cope with day to day living in the modern world. It's an incapacity to function. At all.... You cannot imagine what it takes to feign normalcy, to show up to work, to make a dentist appointment, to pay bills, to walk your dog, to return library books on time, to keep enough toilet paper on hand, when you are exerting most of your capacity on trying not to kill yourself.... Depression is real. Just because you've never had it doesn't make it imaginary. Compassion is also real. And a depressed person may cling to it until they are out of the woods, and they may remember your compassion for the rest of their lives as a force greater than their depression.*

That description so skillfully illustrates what depression can do to people and what it can feel like.

After my back-to-back episodes at sixteen years of age, I had to deal with some serious depressions. Then, after my third episode in the summer of 2004, I met depression again.

In reflecting on that summer, I think it's logical to entertain the idea that my depression was exacerbated because I was still taking only half of my regular dose of Wellbutrin, compliments of Dr. Natasha. Whatever the reason, there were many times when I just didn't want to exist. I would dream of suicide, anything that would allow me to escape the reality that I now lived in. I wanted to do it. Unfortunately, I knew I could never do that to my family. This proved to be a double-edged sword, for knowing that I would never commit suicide made me more depressed, as there was no way out of the pain.

I cried in the shower almost daily. I held back my tears until I was in the shower, because nobody could hear me crying with the water running. I remember one day when I decided to take a bath. I sat there, staring at a razor. Part of me begged myself to use it. I picked up the razor and put it in my hand. All I needed was just two deep cuts, and the pain would be over.

"Do it," I said to myself. "Just do it." I stared at my hands, willing them to move. I wanted to do it, but could not lift the muscles of my hand. It felt odd, as if angels were holding my hands down. I put down the razor and sobbed.

# the decision to fight

My recovery wasn't happening as fast as I wanted, and I felt like giving up. I had hoped that after a few months I would be back at work feeling great. I was so far away from that. Manic thoughts were still lingering, alternating with the depression. I was still confused. I was scared. I had this mental fog that felt like it would never go away. I didn't have anything to live for. I didn't feel like myself. The manic episode was always on my mind. It was a traumatic experience and it haunted me. It was devastating waking up every morning and still feeling uncomfortable in my own skin. Not being able to financially support myself was crushing and added to the snowballing depression.

I was experiencing the same hopelessness that I'd felt after my episodes as a teenager. Back then, after I got home from the hospital, my mom would come into my room and pray with me every night. One night she said something that I will never forget. She looked at me and said, "Margaret, you're like an athlete, and you're just injured right now. Every day you're going to get a little better, until you are completely healed." That was a very powerful statement. It gave me encouragement at the time that I needed it the most.

Now, at twenty-six, I needed to find that encouragement again. But as an adult, things seemed too difficult. It had been almost four months since my episode, and I still felt awful. My family and friends had all gone back to life as usual. When was I going to be better? When could I go back to my life? On television shows like *Oprah* or *Dr. Phil* they feature stories about people who've gone through difficult experiences. You hear about the terrible events, and then how they overcame them. Now that they're on the show, of course, they are officially recovered. The show often illustrates this recovery by showing the survivors walking on the beach, often tossing balls or sticks for their dogs. Now those events are behind them. The beach walk symbolizes that they're fully recovered, they're over their terrible experiences and are living great new lives. I kept asking myself, when was my walk on the beach going to happen? I had survived, hadn't I? Every time I went on a walk, I wished there were cameras following me around showing the world I had recovered. For now, it was just me.

I spent hours smoldering in anger and frustration. I was angry with myself for succumbing to mania. I was angry at my job for helping to put me in this situation. I was angry at society for making me feel so unwanted. I was angry with my family for not understanding me. I was angry with my doctors for treating me like I was broken.

The anger threatened to overtake me. I wanted to blame someone and get justice. For a while it was my job that I blamed the most. I had been fine for ten years. I'd performed in many high-stress jobs and situations and had excelled. But the stress that employees faced at this job was unreasonable and unfair, and I wanted to hold someone accountable. I couldn't move past it. And now I had all this paperwork to deal with, disability applications, insurance claims, bills that piled up while I was gone, endless forms that I had to fill out.

Part of the anger about my job was justified. They had demanded that employees row down the river but had failed to provide them with the oars. However, they weren't really an evil corporation. My illness was fueling these extreme perceptions. I would spend time plotting how I would make a movie about this "evil" corporation and bring it down. I have never felt that much anger about anything in my life. I had a right to be frustrated, even angry, about the job, but the amount of anger I felt was not normal. Those negative emotions were not who I really was. They were merely symptoms of the illness.

My family saw my anger, and worked hard to help me control it. Every time I'd go on a rant about the "evil corporation," my sister would distract me. It was hard for me to focus on anything positive. I was constantly thinking to myself, "I should have prevented this episode. I should have been stronger. I should be *normal.*" It became an endless cycle of "should-ing" all over myself. I'd get depressed, and then get more depressed ... because I was depressed. I felt like a failure.

I kept going over and over in my head what had happened. Every day I'd think about my breakdowns, and be consumed with guilt. I kept comparing myself to others. My inner dialogue was incessantly critical. I was like my own Jewish mother. I'd say to myself, in an accent, of course, "Look at your sister. She has a job, and a husband. Why couldn't you have done that?" I kept thinking, wow, I really f— ed up my life, again.

Then one weekend my attitude shifted. It was Labor Day weekend, a warm, sunny couple of days that meant time off and gorgeous weather and beautiful sunsets. I had just moved in with my sister and her husband in Woodland, California. Despite the sunny time of year, I was feeling rotten, like a juvenile delinquent who'd been forced to stay with his grandparents because he'd totally messed things up and couldn't live at home.

My sister and her husband were away, so I was alone for the weekend. Everybody I knew was out having fun, but not me. I couldn't go out. I still wasn't comfortable in social situations, and I was feeling depressed. I couldn't do the social chitchat that was standard at holiday parties and events. I didn't want to be around anybody.

I drove to Berkeley, about an hour and a half away, to go to a bookstore that I used to frequent before the hospitalization. For some reason I felt safe at that bookstore, and I would do anything to feel safe and normal. On the drive back to Woodland, a tidal wave of anger rose up within me. I was done with feeling bad. I had had enough.

I started yelling at myself. I said to myself (I will put it in all caps so you can get the intensity of the moment), "THAT'S IT, MAGGIE!! THAT'S IT! WE ARE DONE FEELING BAD. WE ARE DONE WITH IT! YOU ARE GOING TO GET YOUR LIFE BACK! YOU ARE NOT DOING THIS ANYMORE. DO YOU HEAR ME? YOU ARE STRONGER THAN THIS. WE ARE GETTING OUR LIFE BACK, AND WE'RE GETTING IT BACK RIGHT NOW!"

I really did that. For about ten minutes, right there on the I-80 freeway going through the East Bay, I yelled at myself. I screamed at myself. With the car rolling and the warm breeze lifting my hair up off my shoulders, I yelled and yelled. It felt great. My strength had been buried deep within layers and layers of difficult emotion, but now it had finally ripped free.

For as long as I could remember I'd wanted to blame somebody for my suffering. Anybody. Society for making me feel ashamed of who I was. People who had criticized me or humiliated me for an illness that I had little or no control over. And now I blamed my employer for making me feel inadequate and making me miss my brother's wedding. I felt sorry for myself, for being a victim of such negative stigma. Poor me.

Every time I looked at myself, I saw someone broken beyond repair. Then I started to realize ... wait a minute. If I couldn't separate my identity from my illness, *how could anyone else?* Nobody was forcing me to feel bad about myself for my diagnosis of mental illness. I, and only I, had the power to accept the reality of the illness, and only I had the power to choose how I would react to it. What a crazy idea.

That moment, and that one realization, changed my life. If I wanted to get better, I would need to fight for it.

# maggie newcomb, f! yeah!

The anger that pulled the words from my throat as I drove through the East Bay, screaming into the air, was incredibly strong. It forced me to make some decisions: I could choose to sit there and stew in the depression and anger, blaming everyone else, or I could choose to move forward. It didn't make the depression go away. Just to be clear, you can't just decide not to be depressed. You can't just "snap out of it." However, I was ready to put in the work to combat the depression. The Rome that my manic mind had created had fallen. I needed to pick up the pieces and rebuild.

Here's the first thing I figured out: the reason my recovery was so slow was because I was holding myself back. Yes, I know that sounds like a Tony Robbins quote, but it was true. If I was so focused on feeling ashamed, how the heck could I move forward? The only way to move forward was to forgive myself and, perhaps more importantly, forgive others. It didn't mean I had to have everything figured out. I wasn't about to forget what had happened to me. It just meant that I needed to release all of the toxic anger so that I could focus on what I was able to do.

I began to see that in order to get where I wanted to be, I had to begin by accepting where I was. Not only where I was, but who I was and what had happened to me. I had a mental condition that I needed to treat in order to function in reality. There was something in my brain that fired too much or too little, and it caused me to be vulnerable to high highs and really low lows. Stress exacerbated the situation. Although I didn't completely understand what had happened with my brain chemistry and the mania I'd fallen into, I knew I'd experienced a major trauma. Let's be honest, I lost my mind. I couldn't just act like nothing happened. You don't just bounce back from that.

I had to start thinking of my situation just like my mom had described it when I was sixteen. I wasn't broken; I was injured. It was as if I had experienced a major physical impairment, like, for instance, I had fallen and broken both my legs. When someone breaks both legs, no one expects that as soon as she gets back up on her feet, she'll immediately be able to go running, or even walk. This is exactly what society expects, though, after someone has a mental breakdown, whether it is mania, depression, or some other form of mental illness. We expect them to pull themselves up by their bootstraps, and get back in there! We expect those with a mental illness to jump back into a life filled with activity, stress and responsibility, back into a crazy world where everyone is running from one thing to the next.

I needed to ignore those expectations. I needed to be patient and block out the stressors from the outside world. I needed to let myself fully heal. That is what someone would do if she broke her legs; she would take time to let them heal completely. *Then,* and only then, would she try to walk. I knew that I needed time; then, once I was stable, I could slowly learn to crawl again or maybe even walk. I couldn't even think about running. So I quit setting time limits on myself. No more continually asking myself, "Am I better yet?" I would do something every day that was healthy and that made me feel whole. That is how I was going to recover. No expectations, just healing.

More important, it was up to me and me alone to create my recovery. So what did I do? I accepted responsibility for the journey. Although I was blessed to have my family and friends supporting me, they couldn't do the work for me. It was up to me to change my life. This recovery had to be fueled by me. And I couldn't do it *for* my family, either; I had to get better for *me*. I wanted to get better, and I believed that is was possible for me to do so. The belief that I could make my recovery happen was the most important recovery tool I had. It was the thing that would carry me to where I wanted to be.

In addition, I realized that my current situation didn't have to define who I was. I could see my present circumstances as merely temporary. Sometimes the hardest part of recovery is that it seems to take forever, and you don't think your circumstances will ever change. I fell back on what I'd learned from my earlier experiences, that this hospitalization did not have to ruin me. I had gotten through two episodes, and I could get through one more. I needed to trust that there was, in fact, a better life for me than the one I was currently living.

Finally, I figured out that focusing on what I wanted rather than what I couldn't control would get me to that better life a lot faster. I still had so many unanswered questions. Had I experienced enlightenment, or was I just crazy? Did I actually go to heaven or just to a mental hospital? As enticing as those questions were, I decided to file them away for future thought, because at that point they didn't matter. What mattered was, what was I going to do to get my life back? How would I get to the place that I wanted to be? I had seen people who'd focused really hard on getting all the answers before they focused on getting help. It never really improved their situation. I had to let go of my need to know everything.

I also needed to let go of my anger at the things I believed had resulted in my present reality. Continually poring over every detail of what had happened to me—the people of my past and recent present, my own behavior and perceived faults, the behavior of others around me—certainly wasn't going to help me move forward. I realized that I could choose to make peace with these things. I could let them all go, so that I could spend my energy on what I needed, and wanted, to do. Exposing the evil of my past job sure wasn't going to get me where I wanted to go. Obsessing about every detail of the situation wasn't going to help me move forward. How many people do you know who seem to complain constantly about how bad things are, and then keep seeing that bad stuff show up in their lives? That wasn't going to be me. I had my eye on the prize. Sanity. And I would get there.

Although I accepted the reality of the situation, I vowed not to accept the limitations that others might place on me. Some might see my mental illness and judge me as inferior, but that sure didn't mean that I needed to agree with their evaluation. Someone else's judgment wasn't going to stop me from living the life that I wanted to live. Just because I accepted my weakness, my illness, didn't mean that I had to let that weakness dictate my life.

One of the most powerful things that I did at that time to take responsibility for my own healing was to confront the situation with my job. I decided to file a workers' compensation claim. Before working with the media research company, I'd been employed at a law firm that specialized in workers' comp, a job known for its high stress and heavy workload, so I knew a little about my rights. Although I did have a preexisting condition, bipolar disorder, that made me more vulnerable to a breakdown, I knew that my job had also greatly contributed to that breakdown. Ironically, despite the insane stress and workload of the workers' comp law firm, I'd never come close to having an episode there.

I filed a claim. I didn't want my former manager to continue to treat people like she had. I did it for myself and, hopefully, for the sake of other workers. The claim was denied. It is very common for workers' compensation psych claims to be denied, as they are very difficult to prove. I was discouraged that it was denied, but I didn't let it get to me. I kept working on myself, and I kept moving forward.

I realized that the life I was moving into would need to be different from the life I'd had before. I couldn't go back to those crazy hours. I couldn't have a job that had unattainable goals. I might have to leave the world of business for a career that was less demanding and stressful. I needed to make some major life changes, ones that would allow mental stability to be my first priority.

Although medication would be an essential part of that stability, it couldn't be the whole enchilada. I would need to add other elements. I couldn't just pop my pills and wait around for them to make me feel all better. I believed that medication could really help with brain chemistry. However, I knew that medication wouldn't fix my life. I had to do it.

I decided to think about the healthy life ahead of me as if it were a new house. I would arrange my house with the things that I liked, things like nice furniture and artwork. I would enjoy spending time in it. However, there would be some upkeep involved. I'd have to organize my space and put things away. I'd need to clean it every once in a while, mop the floors, and give it a quick vacuum. There wasn't one cleaning product that would do the whole job, and I couldn't clean it once and expect it to be clean forever. On the other hand, I could not be expected to be cleaning it all the time. No matter how much time I'd spend scouring it, there would still be dirt somewhere, under a bed or along the baseboards. I would have to be okay with that.

Just like there was a lot that one needed to do to have a nice place to live in, there was a lot that I needed to do to have a life that I would enjoy. Many people are convinced that if they just cure their mental illness they'll be happy. In my opinion, that's not really how it works. I don't think you can cure your mental illness, but you can manage it. I think it's more important to work on creating a *life* that will make you happy. Consequently, when you enjoy your life, your symptoms decrease and your illness is much easier to manage. In the days that followed my cathartic drive through the East Bay, I realized that my mental illness would not be treated in one quick fix. It was going to be an ongoing process.

I was ready to go to work. Cue the 80s montage and play the song *Eye of the Tiger!* Here we go! *F-Yeaahhh!*

# creative treatment

Several months before I'd yelled into the wind, I had developed a treatment plan for my recovery. However, the treatment plan worked much better once I was ready to fully commit to it and accept responsibility for my own healing. When recovering from a mental-illness episode, whether it's depression or mania or any other, you need to look at an entire range of practices, rituals, and activities that can all work together to help you succeed. Medication alone will not get you to where you want to be. There isn't one magic medication. Sure, medications for me were absolutely imperative, but I needed to do many other things in order to recover.

Once I committed, I was very disciplined with my treatment plan. I also decided to get creative with it. In addition to the medication and therapy, I discovered that adding unconventional treatment really seemed to help me.

I started each morning by making a schedule for my day. Since I was home while my friends and family were all at work, I was alone most of the day. At the advice of my sister, I scheduled an hour each day to deal with the mounds of financial and former work-related paperwork that had piled up. Since I knew this could make me frustrated and upset, I only did it for an hour. No matter how much I had to do, I made myself stop. The rest would have to wait until the next day.

I began to go to the gym three times a week. Usually I did cardio for about half an hour, and then did some light weights, pushups, and sit-ups. When I couldn't afford the membership anymore, I would walk for half an hour once a day.

Driving, for some reason, also made me feel better. After I moved to Woodland, I would often drive to the Bay Area several times each week just to cheer myself up. I went to places that I had enjoyed before I'd had my episode. These places reminded me of my old self and gave me physical evidence of the possibility of recovery.

I went to noon mass once in a while. The noon mass at the Catholic church near the campus of the University of California at Berkeley was quiet and peaceful, without many people in attendance. Sometimes I would get there early and just sit. Sometimes I would cry. Some of the sermons were very healing to me. Principles like faith, redemption and resurrection really resonated with me. Although I have problems with some of the doctrines and leaders of Catholicism, I am extremely grateful for this church and for those healing masses.

Bookstores were my favorite safe place. (For you young people, a bookstore is like Amazon or iBooks. But it is a physical store that you actually have to walk into and possibly even interact with another human being.) Something about being in a bookstore like Barnes and Noble or Borders just felt good. I would walk around for a bit, looking at all the inspirational covers. Sometimes I would hang out in the New Age section and read about other people's spiritual enlightenment. Or I would sit in the self-help section and read about other people's recovery from loss. These accounts made me feel less alone and even inspired. I would sit for hours skimming through books.

Nordstrom was another safe place, because it reminded me of my grandmother. I couldn't afford to buy anything, but I still enjoyed myself. I would go to the café and get an iced tea or diet coke and pretend I was with my grandmother, whom I still felt so close to.

Sometimes I would look at clothes and then picture how I would feel wearing them, a new life in great new clothes!

I took several trips to Stinson Beach and watched the water breaking off the shore. I also walked around Lake Merritt and along Crissy Field. The spectacular views, the waterfront, the wildlife, all of the beauty distracted me from how I was really feeling. When I walked on the beach, I still looked around for cameras. None yet, but I knew I was close.

Music was by far the best medicine for me. Whenever I started to get scared or depressed, I would put on music and let it take me to another place. One day I went to Berkeley and bought several CDs that I knew would make me feel better. I bought Tom Jones, George Michael, Prince and some jazz. There was a song by George Michael called "Amazing" that really touched me. I would play the CD over and over while driving. For a few weeks it was the only song that I listened to. I must have listened to it hundreds of times. I pretended like it was God singing to me that I was amazing.

Sometimes I would lie on my bed listening to music. I would lift my arms in the air as if I were conducting the band, or move my fingers as if playing the piano. I would do that for hours. I also took long baths and brought the CD player into the bathroom. I would sit there in the bath and listen to jazzy blues CDs like those by Etta James. Sometimes when in the bath I would turn off the music and lie back so my ears were underwater and my eyes were out of the water. All noise was shut out. Underwater it was complete silence. Peaceful. I would lay there in that peace for as long as I could, staring up at the ceiling.

Dancing in my room while listening to upbeat music became another important recovery tool. Anything that would take my mind off of what I perceived to be the reality of my situation. I would blare hip-hop, old-school Michael Jackson, Prince, Stevie Wonder. I danced around my room like nobody's business. I mean, I would really shake it. Like a Polaroid picture.

I would also spend hours lying in my sister's backyard, staring at the sky. The grass felt nice underneath me. The blue sky with the puffy while clouds was somehow soothing, as if it represented another world above. My backyard ritual reminded me that even if I hadn't made it to heaven, heaven was still there. My sister and her husband found it a little odd that I would just lie in the cool grass and stare at the sky, but they wanted to be supportive so they didn't say anything.

I spent a lot of time taking care of my body. When I was slightly manic a few months earlier, I'd bought some expensive, natural body-care products. Normally I would never spend this kind of money, but I was glad that I had, because in my recovery it seemed important. I would take part in serious beauty rituals, the kind of things that I would never do before. I would have "pretty princess" baths. I would exfoliate and shave. I saw my body as a temple, and I wanted to cherish it. (Nowadays I'm lucky if I shave my legs once a week. Just ask my boyfriend.)

Journaling and drawing were two other activities that I also gravitated to quite a lot. During the months of my recovery, I filled several notebooks. Many times I would sit in the backyard or in the living room that overlooked it. For a while I would write about my situation and about the manic thoughts that were slowly fading from my awareness. The philosophies of life that still lingered in my mind poured onto the paper. In addition, I drew many colorful pictures with colored pencils that my mom got me. Some pictures would be of the scenery around me, a basket of fruit or flowers in the garden. Other times they would be completely abstract, like colorful collages. Those times were special to me. Somehow the act of journaling, in particular, made me feel less alone.

Reading positive books also helped. I pulled out some of my classic favorites, like *Seat of the Soul* by Gary Zukav.

I added a healthy routine and some non-traditional medicine to my recovery plan. I saw a chiropractor on a regular basis. I decided I wouldn't drink alcohol for a year. I ate healthily and drank plenty of water. I got over eight hours of sleep at night. I started some light meditation. This time I was careful so that the meditation would not consume me, as it had the last time.

I eventually volunteered at a care facility for older adults. After a few visits, though, I had to stop. It was a little depressing, and I wasn't quite ready for that yet.

All these things that I was doing were starting to help, even if they just helped me live another day. I knew that I needed to keep busy. If I didn't keep moving and I stopped to look around at where I was and where I had been, it became frightening. My family and friends constantly reminded me that this situation was just temporary. I needed to keep moving forward, by every day doing something good for myself. When my sister saw me she would say, "You're doing it! You're doing it!" It was sort of our little joke. "Doing it" meant doing anything other than wallowing in depression or giving in to manic rants. It was so tough yet so simple at the same time: just by wanting to get better, I was "doing it." I hoped and prayed that what I was doing would pay off.

I believe that what helped my recovery most was doing stand-up comedy. Rather than focusing on my episode or the speed of my recovery, I began to write comedy. I wrote and re-wrote my jokes. My act was constantly going through my head; when driving, showering, or working out at the gym, my mind was focused on the jokes. The same mind that used to race was now, once again, working for good. Pacing in the backyard was a normal event, as I practiced my sets.

In late September, I felt I was ready to try stand-up in public again. I went to the Sacramento Punch Line Open Mic. Once a month they had an open mic for amateurs. I practiced my seven-minute set all day long. I decided to go back to the basics by using the old jokes that I'd started with. Nothing about bipolar disorder or mental hospitals. I wasn't ready for that.

I got to the club early to sign up. Luckily I ran into a comic I'd met the year before at a comedy competition. He was a hilarious

African-American male in his mid-twenties, and he had the kind of smile that lit up the room. When he saw me he said, "Hey girl, I think I've met you before. What was your name again?"

"Maggie," I replied. "We met at the comedy competition in Sunnyvale several months ago."

"That's right," he said. "I haven't seen you in a while. Where have you been?" I didn't know what to say. Should I blurt out that I was in a mental hospital? Probably not very cool.

"You know, just sort of taking a break."

He smiled. "I hear that."

Then I asked, "Um, so, how do I sign up for the open mic?"

"I can help you with that," he replied. "I'm the MC. I'll make sure you get on the list."

I was so relieved that he was being nice to me. There are open mics in some cities that are ruthless. Everybody wants stage time, but there are only so many spots in the show. It's every comic for himself. The Sacramento comedy scene was different. Everyone supported each other.

He took me to the back of the club, where all the other comics were sitting. "Hey guys, this is Maggie. She's a funny lady I met in the Bay last year." The comics greeted me, and then went on looking at their sets. It was a very diverse group, Latinos, African-Americans, Asians and white guys. I was, however, the only girl. Maybe that's why they were being so nice to me.

I was beyond nervous. As I waited to go on, I resisted the urge to pace back and forth in the greenroom. Then the MC called me up.

I walked to center stage and took the microphone out of the stand. My hand shook a little. I looked out at the crowd, and was immediately blinded by the spotlight in my eye. I blinked for a second and then went into the routine that I'd been practicing all day.

"So one of the things that I hate about being single: everyone is always trying to set you up. My sister called me the other day and said, 'Maggie we have the *perfect* guy for you.' 'Why is he perfect?' I asked. 'Well ...' she said, 'he's single and you're single.'"

Pause and laugh. Phew, they laughed! I thought. Then I added, "Now I know how Ling Ling the panda feels." Pause … and a bigger laugh. I was so relieved.

The rest of the set went okay. I got a couple of laughs. I messed up my closer. It wasn't perfection, but I didn't bomb. The important thing was that I actually *did* it. It must not have been as bad as I thought, because many of the comics came up to me and said they loved my set. Again, this may have been because I was the only girl. I didn't care; it was just nice to get a positive reaction. And that was just the beginning.

Now that I was able to do stand-up again, I had something truly positive to focus on. Every day my mental health got better and better.

I was exiting crazytown and re-entering the real world.

# the new doctor

In all the years I'd received treatment for my illness, doctors had always been appointed for me. Either my parents, the university, or the hospital had chosen them. I had never been asked about the decision. I appreciated the professional treatment I received and am extremely grateful for it, but I never really connected with any of the doctors. I felt that each time they worked with me they only saw an illness that they needed to treat. They didn't really see *me*. The attitude I got from them was that I was broken or flawed and they needed to "fix" me. I ended up feeling more judged than healed.

When I had to get a new doctor in Northern California, I wasn't sure what to do. It had been a while since I'd seen my doctor in the hospital and I needed to renew my prescriptions. I went to my insurance company website and started researching doctors who were in my network. I made phone calls to three of them and left messages to see if they were taking new patients.

The first doctor to call me back was Doctor Shoreman. He sounded very nice and calm on the phone. The other two who called me back sounded busy and important. I'd been there and done that, so I decided to listen to my gut and go with Doctor Shoreman. I will never forget my first visit with him.

I chose a doctor in the Bay Area since, at that time, the Bay Area was the place that I wanted to eventually live. Dr. Shoreman's office was located in the Marina District of San Francisco, off Union Street. It was in an old, remodeled Victorian house. Many office buildings in that part of town were like this. I walked up the first-floor stairs and sat down in the lobby. I tried to calm my nerves.

A man in his sixties came out of his office to greet me. He had gray hair, was slightly overweight, and wore a gray suit. My nervousness started to dissipate. He looked at me and said, "Well, hello there. Are you Miss Maggie Newcomb?"

"Uh, yes," I said.

"I'm Dr. Shoreman. Come on into my office."

I followed him down the hall and into his office, which overlooked the busy Marina district. He took a seat at a small table by the window, then directed me to a large chair that faced the table. As I stood by the chair I looked around. There were teddy bears everywhere! There must have been close to a hundred of them. They were all very detailed and unique. Some with clothes, some with glasses, some that were different colors. Every type of bear you could imagine was in this man's room. Small and intricate to big and fuzzy.

"Don't mind the bears," he said, following my gaze. "They won't hurt you." Then he smiled with a warmth that reminded me of my grandfather. Normally I would find teddy bears in a grown man's office to be weird. But it seemed to work for him. He had a gentle, welcoming quality, and the bears were part of the package.

He started first. "Well, it's very nice to meet you. I have an important question for you ..."

Here we go, I thought. The mental health questions, and the judgment. Then he continued.

"What happened when two peanuts walked down the street?" He looked earnestly at me, waiting for an answer.

"Um ... I don't know."

He quickly responded, "One was a-salted!" He immediately laughed, a rich, warm, friendly laugh. Then I laughed too.

I was no longer nervous.

"I just love that one," he said. "So simple." He looked down at my file. Then he looked back at me. "On the phone you mentioned that you have bipolar I disorder and that you just had a manic episode. Is that right?"

"Yes," I replied. "I got out of the hospital not too long ago."

He said, "You know, I find people with bipolar disorder so fascinating! I've been working with them for over thirty years."

Fascinating? I had never met a doctor who thought I was fascinating. Then he went on.

"You know, I worked with a physician who was so manic one time that he bought a helicopter! He didn't even know how to fly it!" We both laughed. It wasn't like he was judging this bipolar doctor; he was more in awe. This was such a new perspective for me.

"So, my dear. Can you tell me about what you've gone through?"

I started talking about what happened, from the very beginning. He listened attentively, as if every word I said was valuable. He jotted down many notes. Every once in a while he would ask a question to clarify something. When the hour was almost up, I stopped talking. I waited for the judgment of what I should or shouldn't be doing. Instead I got a totally different response.

"Well, you've been through quite a lot. It looks like you're handling it quite well."

It was the strangest response I had ever received. He didn't tell me what was wrong with me. To the contrary, judging from his response to my story, he almost admired what I'd been through. I was so surprised at his reaction that I didn't know what to say.

Luckily, he went on. "Don't you worry. If you ever get manic again, I know exactly what to do. Medications are getting so good that you just call me when you're feeling manic, and we will nip it right in the bud. My main concern is that you remain stable and don't get depressed."

Nip "it" in the bud. Wait, what was he saying? That there was a difference between my illness and me? Like, maybe what had happened wasn't my fault at all. "It" was to blame. He seemed so calm, so matter of fact. Like mania was just a nuisance that had to be dealt with. Deep inside somewhere, years of shame started to fall away.

Then he asked, "Are you feeling at all depressed?"

I replied, "Yes, I am."

"Hmm," he said. "Why do you think that is?"

He was genuinely interested in *my* opinion. "Many reasons. My situation. It also may be because my Wellbutrin is half of what it had been for ten years. My last doctor in the hospital lowered it so I wouldn't get manic."

He looked surprised. "That's an interesting approach. Did you feel better at your old dosage?"

"Yes," I said.

"Well, I think we should go back to that dose. Don't you?" I had never had a doctor consult with me about my meds; they'd always made the decisions for me.

"Uh, yes. I do."

He took out his prescription pad. "Okay, then let me just write that up for you."

It took us several sessions for me to talk about everything I'd been through. I felt I was getting years of pain off my chest. Throughout the sessions he never told me what to do. He just listened, hanging onto my every word. He was genuinely trying to get to know *me*. When I finished explaining my life story, Dr. Shoreman sat for a minute and took it all in.

"You've had quite an impressive life, young lady. I think that you are on the right track!"

His supportive and joking personality was so healing for me. After I'd been seeing him for a few years he said one day, "I don't understand why you don't have a boyfriend yet. You are such a nice girl."

"I don't know either," I replied.

"Hmm," he said softly. Then his face lit up. "I have an idea!" He pulled out his prescription pad and started writing. He tore it off and handed it to me with a smile.

"What's this?" I asked.

He responded with confidence. "It's a prescription for a loving and supportive boyfriend. So go out there and find one." Then he laughed. Unfortunately, I wasn't able to fill that script right away. Eventually, though, I did.

Dr. Shoreman became more of a friend, or even like a close relative. I saw him every week for several months. Then we went to every other week. Then every several weeks. He was just nice to me. We'd spend many of our sessions telling each other jokes. When I told him that I was going to get back into stand-up, he was overjoyed. He loved that I did stand-up. He even came to one of my comedy shows. And I, in turn, felt safe with him. Just by listening and being supportive, he slowly helped build up the confidence I needed to re-enter my life.

With my medication back to its normal dose, I noticed a significant difference in my moods. It became easier and easier for me to get through the day. If it wasn't for him and his unique, caring treatment, I would not have been ready for some pretty incredible opportunities ahead.

# crazy or enlightened?

Now that my professional treatment and healthy lifestyle were in full effect, I had some soul searching to do. Although I accepted that I needed treatment for my mental instability, I still didn't fully understand what the heck had happened. Who was I? Was I crazy, or was I spiritually enlightened? Was God really speaking to me? Did I go to heaven? Or was I just mentally ill?

As I reflected back on the last few months, part of me didn't want to forget those thoughts, the feelings, and the dreams that had fueled my life and fed my soul in those days when my mania was at its height. It wasn't just that a lot of new ideas came into my mind; it was the awareness that I had entered a new phase of consciousness. This new consciousness made so much sense and was so exciting, and was accompanied by such a sense of knowingness and certainty, that it overtook my rational mind. The feelings that came along with the thoughts were even more powerful. They were indescribable in language, but words like "bliss" and "excitement" begin to capture what I felt. It was what I imagined heaven would feel like. Even though months had gone by and that manic intensity was gone, the memories of everything I'd experienced during that manic time were so vibrant in my mind.

When I was manic, enlightenment came in two forms. I understood and realized many things that I accepted as my beliefs, and these intellectual realizations inspired strong feelings and emotions. The intellectual and the emotional together created a sort of nirvana experience. By this I mean, I didn't just have a *knowing* of enlightenment, I also *felt* it as a reality. For instance, I realized that time had no meaning, and I also experienced it. I believed that human beings are, by their nature, supposed to feel good, and my positive emotions and senses were heightened. I accepted that we are all beautiful in our own unique way, and I felt extremely attractive. I knew that money was just an energy source, and I gave it away freely. I knew that God could speak with us all, and I experienced God speaking directly to me, loving me unconditionally. I also had overwhelming feelings of love and my social consciousness was heightened. I felt strongly connected to everything and everyone.

All of the phenomena that I experienced were similar to those referred to in many Eastern and Western cultures as experiences of enlightenment, experiences that have been documented for hundreds of years. Eastern religions and philosophies speak of the nirvana of Buddhism, and the Hindu concept of oneness. Western religion speaks of the mystical experiences of Christian saints, the spirituality of the New Thought movement, and more.

When I looked at some of the history, it seemed unfair. When certain people claimed to have had experiences of enlightenment, they were regarded as experts or worshipped as saints. Yet when I and others like me tried to express the same things, we were discounted. Were we ignored, laughed at or locked away because so many of us have difficulty clearly expressing the experiences we have when we're manic? Or does society just totally reject any kind of comparison between a person considered mentally ill and someone considered worthy of enlightenment? Is enlightenment only taken seriously if someone wears a robe or a habit or a miter?

I have struggled with these questions ever since my first episode at the age of sixteen. For a young person struggling with issues of identity and self-image, the added confusion over the nature of what

I'd experienced only added to my pain. I searched for the right answer for almost two decades, and have now arrived at a question of my own: what if there isn't just one answer? What if I get to choose the answers that are correct for me? I mean, if famous people like Madonna and Prince get to choose their names, shouldn't I be able to choose what I believe in? I would like to create the gray area that I choose to live in, rather than the extremes. What if I am not just one thing—crazy, sane or enlightened? What if I am all three? What if I get to decide who I am?

Although I was diagnosed with a mental illness, I came to the conclusion that there was nothing wrong with me, or, as the New Thought maxim says, I was born whole, perfect and complete. I believe that there is some sort of energy or source that has created everything we see, call it God, nature, Mother Earth, Love, Buddha, David Hasselhoff, whatever. I call this energy God, and sometimes I think that God made me with an unbalanced mind that is vulnerable to destructive highs and devastating lows because maybe, just maybe, there is something unique for me to learn in this journey. God invented science. God *made* the scientists who discovered the distinct range of medications that are available to me.

I still had questions, though, about the state of mania itself. Is mania—by its nature—good, or bad? Most people, myself included, love the experience of mania when it creates passion and focus and a spiritual enlightenment. It's like taking really awesome drugs for free. But an enlightenment that was so clear and vivid and logical had, in each case, transformed into something truly awful. Why did it start off in ecstasy but morph into nightmares? Why did my mind take me to such terrifying places? Why did I fall into a horrible depression at the end of each episode? Was the only lesson to be learned that "The higher you go, the harder you fall"?

I do not know the answers, but here is what I now know. Mania can be absolutely amazing at times, and I wouldn't trade the experience for anything. But as much as I love being richly creative and feeling spiritually enlightened, I can't live there *all* the time. What good is being enlightened if you don't have anyone to share it with? What good is being enlightened if you can't even support yourself? I choose to live in the real world with my family and friends, and in the real world one needs to eat, sleep, bathe, and take care of oneself. One needs to get up every day and go to work to be able to pay for all of this eating and sleeping and bathing. It's impossible to function in reality while you are highly manic.

In the years following my third episode, I decided to safely experiment with some of the ideas I'd had when I was manic. I began to pull some of the insights and realizations I experienced and reshape them so that I could practice them in actual reality. I hypothesized that I could accept and even implement the basic beliefs, but on a much smaller scale, so that they did not take over my life. Since I saw money as energy, I began to be responsibly generous. No more tipping waitresses $50, but tipping well, nonetheless. In various ways, I practiced being socially conscious. I opened myself to feeling love and expressing love freely. I continued to build my relationship with the all-loving source, which for me, I call God. I communicated with God through prayer and meditation, however, with the understanding that I was no different than anyone else. In my opinion, we are all magnificent beings; too many of us are just not aware of it.

I also discovered that I can reach moments of enlightenment at certain times in my everyday life, without letting it distort reality. When I am creating, laughing with friends, performing on stage, exercising, meditating, petting an animal, loving, you name it—I am in a special place. That place can be called enlightenment, the creative zone, a peak experience, or any other name that feels right. The title isn't important. What's important is that you stop and realize that you are in it. These feelings of enlightenment are within our reach as we live our everyday lives. Everyone has access to them. You don't have to get manic to feel them. More important, they don't have to take over your life.

I think that what happens to many of the people who have an untreated mental illness is that they slip into a mania or psychosis and feel as if they're more enlightened or more connected to God, and they don't know how to come back. Maybe they don't have anything to come back to. Maybe they don't have a family and resources, like I did. They don't have anybody to help them come back to reality. I also believe it is possible that the longer you stay manic, the harder it is to come back. Many people stuck in their intense mania end up on the streets, living in their delusions. After many episodes of this, they don't know how to function in our world anymore. I don't blame them. Delusions are so powerful.

Contemplating the question of craziness vs. enlightenment ultimately took me to the question of what I believe about an afterlife. I still believe in heaven, but as I mentioned earlier I have come to believe that it isn't a physical place, but is more like a shift in consciousness or maybe even a different dimension. I think the spectacular, spiritually enlightening highs of mania that I experienced might be what heaven is like. Heaven is probably even better, but as a human I am unable to comprehend the extent of its splendor. I still believe we can go to heaven when we die, but I also think we can experience it on earth. When manic, I was only able to grab just a slight taste of it, but, for those delicious minutes, I was in heaven. We all have the opportunity to have heavenly moments. This happens more often whenever we realize our connection to something bigger than our own ego.

Since my manic realizations about heaven, I do not fear death at all. I know we will be taken to a place with incredible feelings that are beyond our comprehension. To be honest, there are days that I look forward to death, as morbid as that sounds. At times I feel like I'm imprisoned by my own brain and my own limitations, and, at those times, life can feel like hell. Sometimes, when I'm feeling like that, I remember those moments of mania, those brief glimpses of what it feels like to let go of all my inhibitions and self-doubt. Man, it's amazing. I will get there again one day when it's my time, I just know it. I am not in charge of the "when." At least, though, I got a taste of heaven while here on Earth.

Maybe God really was speaking to me in my manic episodes. Just because I have a mental illness doesn't mean God can't speak to me. Illness is a part of life that He/She/It created. I can have an illness and be spiritual at the same time. Moreover, I think God talks to all of us; we just don't have time to listen.

Ellen DeGeneres, one of my personal heroes, has a great bit about God in one of her stand-up comedy shows. In her act she is talking to God on the phone. She wants to know why there are terrible things on earth, like fleas. Fleas only seem to cause harm, why would we need them? While pretending to hold a phone to her head she asks God, "There are certain things on this earth, I just don't understand why they are here. . . . I was thinking more about fleas. They seem to have no benefit." We see that God answers her question, and she replies, "No, I didn't realize how many people were employed by the flea collar industry." Then there is a loud laugh from the crowd. This, to me, means that, although we may not see it, there is meaning in the things that we think are bad. This speaks to me on many levels. We are so ingrained in our thinking about what is good or bad, crazy or enlightened, that we often can't see any other perspective. There are so many ways that we can look at mania, its unpredictability, its boundless energy, its agitations, its indescribable highs. There are so many ways that we can look at mental illness in general. Perhaps the wisest way is to bring forward our compassion, our empathy and, most important, our sense of humor.

I think that in the distant future, maybe not even in my lifetime, our society will see that mental illness isn't an illness at all but just a different way of living and experiencing life. We will understand the mind and body a little better. Mental illness is a state of mind that differs from the reality that others experience. Those with this condition will be taught how to live in society that thinks differently from them. They will learn coping mechanisms to exist with stability and techniques to enjoy their gifts. Perhaps people like me won't need to take medication anymore. We will learn to value what is different rather than be afraid of it.

I see mental illness as a kind of inconvenient enlightenment. A person is pulled from the reality of everyday life in order that he or she might have the opportunity to look and to see things differently. That person may suffer along the way, but suffering, depending upon which religion or philosophy you follow, is also considered to be an important part of enlightenment. Many people in both the East and the West believe that it is through suffering that we are given the ability to experience enlightenment. You can't have one without the other. So I accept the exciting, enlightening part of mania, as well as the dark parts and everything in between.

Now with all that being said, I have to be real for a second. I truly believe deep in my heart all that I just wrote. But let's be honest, I don't always live it. I try. I do try. Many days I feel crazy or stupid or lazy or weird. You name it. There is a battle going on in my head every day, trying to find "normal." The conditions around me can affect me more than I would like. When the house is messy, work gets stressful, or relationships get tough, I do not feel enlightened. In those moments I am learning to pause, accept it and see it as temporary. I get through it. Then every once in a while something small happens, a caring gesture from a stranger, a funny TV show, a hug from a friend, a kiss from my boyfriend or a big piece of chocolate with peanut butter. I get glimpses of the enlightenment and that gives me the strength to keep on going.

We are all flawed in different and unique ways. It is what makes us human. There is something beautiful about being human. It's okay to be at rock bottom, it's okay to need help. It is part of the human experience to overcome hardship. To learn from the pain. Sometimes you have to completely break before you can rebuild.

All my experiences, all that I had been through, the highs and the lows, helped pave the way for what was about to happen next.

# the comedy contest

In October of 2004, six months after my episode, I entered a comedy contest. Since I'd stuck with my new doctor, my medications and my creative treatment plan for the past several months, I was ready. I had been slowly adding more stand-up comedy along the way, performing in smaller venues in places in the Bay Area and Sacramento.

The contest I entered was called the Battle of the Bay. It was a yearly comedy competition in the Bay Area put on by the San Francisco Comedy College. The finals were held at the San Jose Improv that year. The Improv is a comedy chain with locations all over the country, and in the comedy world it is a highly respected chain. The San Jose Improv is one of the best comedy venues in all of Northern California. It seats around 450 people on two levels. With its red carpet and red velvet seats, it is quite impressive. As a comic I was in awe of it. It was a long way away from that back room of the coffee shop in Berkeley. It felt like being in a legendary church. It was like the Vatican. It was big time for me.

Over 100 comics had entered that year's competition. There were four heats in the tournament (the preliminary round, the quarter finals, the semi-finals and the finals). About ten comics competed in each series of rounds, and only the top two or three in each round advanced to the next level. The first one, the preliminary round, was in October. I really didn't expect to advance. I just wanted the practice. We had to have seven minutes of material, the same amount as the set I'd done my first time at the coffee shop in Berkeley.

I invited all my friends to the preliminary round. Luckily, all my practicing paid off. All the pacing in my sister's back yard was not for nothing. I did way better than I had expected. I got first and advanced to the quarterfinal round. With the high from the win, comedy became the driving force in my life. I wrote new jokes every day.

For the quarterfinal round we had to do ten minutes. I prepared my set and went to that night's performance with an open mind. I chose to keep it interesting, with different jokes than the preliminary round. I was voted one of the top three comics and advanced again.

Then it was the semifinal round in November, and I needed to do twelve minutes. Comics all around me were being cut, but I was still there. I prepared my twelve minutes of material, practicing countless times a day. Again, I tried to do different material than the other two rounds. To my surprise the audience really liked my performance and I was voted into the top three. I had advanced to the final round at the San Jose Improv!

Before I knew it, it was December of 2004, and I was in the finals of the Battle of the Bay. Out of many comics, I had remained. I needed to have fifteen minutes of material prepared. What? This was crazy. How did I get here? I had never done fifteen minutes straight through before. I was pretty sure it was a fluke that I was in the finals. I would choose my best material for this show. My only goal was to just not come in last place.

As I'd made my way through each round of the Battle of the Bay competition, I was petrified. The part of comedy that made me the most nervous was walking up to the mic, taking the mic out of the stand, and saying the first line of my set. To help with that I used imagery and visioning techniques that I had learned when I was a rower. In the two weeks that preceded the finals I practiced these techniques every night. I would lie in my bed, close my eyes, and visualize myself walking on stage and pulling the mic out of the stand, feeling calm and relaxed as I did so. Then I would see myself going through the different steps of my performance, feeling calm and confident throughout. My ritual seemed to help: the fear slowly dissipated.

My family and friends were very excited for me. I think they were a little surprised at how far I'd come in so little time. Many of them came to my shows and cheered me on.

I arrived early on the night of the finals. I walked into the Improv and looked at all the empty seats that would soon be filled with people. I met with the MC and the comics in the greenroom. We had to draw cards out of a hat to see what order we'd be performing in. I chose the number seven. Lucky number 7, I thought.

About an hour before I was about to go up, I took a pill that would stop my hands from shaking. A few months earlier I'd found out that Lithium made my hands shake on stage. Really uncool for a comic. I talked to Dr. Shoreman and he prescribed a medication that fixed it. It was just a simple blood-pressure medication, but it did the trick.

I talked with some of the other comics for a bit. Talking with comics is always so enjoyable. I feel like I am with my people. We're all a little crazy, and we're not afraid to talk about our emotional baggage. Most important, with comics you never have to do any of that BS banter. None of the "How are you?" or "So, what do you do?" Comics get right to the point. "I feel like crap" or "Hey, this show sucks" or "Did you see the rack on that lady in the front row?" are typical topics among comics. You can talk about anything. Many comics drink and smoke to deal with their pre-performance nerves. I don't like to do either. I spent most of the time before the show in the hallway near the greenroom upstairs, performing my usual pre-show ritual of pacing back and forth while I went over my act in my head.

A lot of my family and friends were there. I really wanted to do well. I didn't want to embarrass them. But I was so nervous. I mean, who did I think I was? What was I *doing* there?

When the MC finally called me to the stage, I was as ready as I'd ever be. Just like I'd practiced in my mind for the last several weeks, I strolled onto the stage, with a strange feeling of calm and confidence. The stage lights shone brightly in my face. I was wearing faded jeans and a long-sleeve black shirt. Nothing tight or sexy. My hair was pulled back into a ponytail, and I wore my Liz Lemon glasses as an added touch. The audience was dark and quiet.

I did the typical comic opener: "What a great crowd we have here tonight!" The audience cheered, with my friends and family probably cheering the loudest. I went on. "I'm so excited to be here tonight. I'm not sure if I want you to laugh at my jokes or … hold me." I got a few small laughs. I did a little banter about the competition. Still getting warmed up. Then I went into my set.

I told a story about where I lived and going to bars. It was the setup. Then I threw out the first big punch line! It got a great laugh from the crowd! It felt good. Then I went on to my other jokes. I did the setup, then the punch line ... and ... wait for it ... bam! The big laughs came. I felt the warmth of the crowd's positive energy flow back at me with every joke. Even in the jokes that were a little racy, I felt no embarrassment. Even though my aunt and uncle were in the audience, I didn't care. It was my moment. I went through my act, joke by joke, and even added a few things in the moment. I was in the groove. And I ended my set with, as we like to call in the biz, a mother f-ing POW!

I had no idea how well I did or how I compared with other comics, but I didn't care. I had risen to the occasion. I made this moment happen and I felt great. There were some amazing comics who performed that night. Comics that had been doing this for almost ten years. One guy from LA had a fantastic bit about prescription-drug side effects. It was genius. I'd only been doing it a year and a half. Eight months earlier I was in a mental hospital drawing pictures about a night like this and being patronized by a counselor. As all Oscar nominees say, I was just happy to be there.

After all the comics had performed, the crowd voted and the judges collaborated. The judges were two of the managers at the San Jose Improv at the time. The final tally would reflect a mix of 50% audience votes and 50% judges. Whoever won would get a cash prize around $1,000 and a weekend MC job at the Improv, opening for a major headliner. Far more than I had ever gotten before.

When the tallies were in, the comics walked on stage to wait for the announcement of the winner. I didn't expect much. At best, I thought I might have a shot at 3rd place. I stood there on stage, with the crowd cheering.

The MC announced the 3rd-place winner, and it wasn't me. I was a little disappointed, but still so happy to have been a part of that competition. I relaxed, knowing that that was it for me. It was a good show to add to my resume. I could go home proud.

Then they said that they had no 2nd place because they had a tie for first place. They announced that the guy from LA had won. Everybody cheered. I wasn't surprised; he had a great set. Then the MC said, "And the other winner is …" He looked at me and said, "Maggie Newcomb!"

I froze. What? *Me?* The mental patient? *What?* No. There must be some sort of mistake, I thought. The audience was going crazy, cheering and screaming. They were cheering for *me?!* It was surreal. They gave me some flowers and a certificate for the cash prize, and I just stood there, more stunned than I'd ever been in my life. With the stage lights shining on me, and in front of the brick-wall background, I stood there, a winner. Okay, maybe I was one of two, but who cares—I was a winner.

And this time it wasn't a dream. It was real.

# my road to recovery

That last chapter would have been a really great place to end this story ... if it were a movie. I drive into the sunset on a cool Harley, my flowers and cash certificate sticking out of my backpack and flapping in the breeze. I spend the rest of my days walking on the beach in my North Face fleece, throwing a stick for my dog, reminiscing about how great life is now and how awful it was before. Reoccurring appearances on *Oprah* for the rest of my life!

Well, that would be nice, but this is reality. I may have been a winner, but a winner still needs to take care of herself, get a job, do laundry, and put pants on—one leg at a time.

In June of 2005, six months after the comedy contest, my disability ended. At that time I was only allowed to be on disability for a year. My doctor said I could appeal it and try to continue receiving disability payments, but I decided not to go that route. I knew it was time for me to move on. It had been a little over a year since I'd had my episode. I hated that I'd been on disability for as long as I had, but doing so was the *most important* factor in my recovery. It had allowed me to completely get over the episode and find true stability. I knew that if I'd gone back to work sooner than I had, I most likely would have relapsed.

I may have looked normal, being able to go to shows and perform stand-up comedy. However, it took at least a year for the ability to cope with reality and handle the stress of supporting myself to come back. As I discussed in my earlier analogy of recovering from two broken legs, having time off from work allowed my brain, and my mind, to heal from the trauma that it had experienced. I had that time to recover without worrying how I was going to eat and survive. Now I was ready to start walking a new path.

I was also able to find closure with my old job. I sought help from the law firm I'd worked at years earlier. I appealed the rejection of my workers' compensation claim. Despite the fact that my illness was a mitigating circumstance in what happened, I still felt that the media research company should have been able see the repercussions of bad management and unethical practices. My action could benefit scores of employees who, like me, were giving their all in order to do a good job.

Then shortly after the disability ended, in July of 2005, I went to court with this former employer. Although they refused to claim any responsibility in what had happened, they offered me a settlement if I officially quit the job. Basically, they just wanted me to go away quietly and never come back. I decided to take the offer. I was tired of the whole thing. The amount was decent, but less than I would have made in a year at that job and I also had to pay several thousand in attorney's fees. The settlement money helped me live for the next couple of years on only a part-time salary. Being able to re-enter the work force on a part-time rather than full-time basis was another factor that allowed me to successfully re-enter the work world and the world at large in the aftermath of my episode.

Through all this, comedy was a major part in my life. Since the comedy contest I continued to do stand-up, which helped my recovery tremendously. Comedy and my recovery became the main focus of my life, and the more I focused on the first, the faster the second one happened. I plain old felt better whenever I was doing stand-up. It consumed me, and I loved every minute of it. All I cared about was stage time and writing new jokes. The only way you become a better comic is getting up on stage as much as you can. Wherever I could get stage time, I would go. I did tons of shows in all kind of places—bars, comedy clubs, dance clubs, street fairs, restaurants, theatres, churches, wineries, coffee shops, laundromats, private houses, casinos, conventions, a retirement community, non-profits, breweries, you name it! Some weeks I got on stage every night. I would even wait for hours at an open mic just to get three minutes. I wasn't getting paid, but I didn't care. On stage is where I felt whole.

In addition to being on stage and writing jokes, I loved spending time with other comics. Although in some towns comics can be jerks, the comics I met in Sacramento and San Francisco were the opposite. They were very supportive and became my family. Comics accept each other: young, old, large, small, white, black, whatever. As I mentioned earlier, none of that surface-level BS matters. Nobody cares what car you drive, where you went to school, or where you live. You don't have to be polite with comics. None of that stupid small talk, which I hate. We know how hard it is to make people laugh so we understand what we each go through. We all have good and bad nights. We give each other feedback about better punchlines or call backs.

Although there are a few comics that are funny all the time, typical class clowns, many comics are pretty mellow, like me. On stage is where we let a different side of ourselves show. Many comics have had or still have difficult lives. Like me, some have had some pretty intense emotional problems, and some have issues with alcohol and drugs. We can laugh at all the hard times. We can laugh at ourselves. We don't have to pretend we are normal. Who wants to be normal anyway?

In July of 2005, I started MCing or hosting shows on the weekends and getting paid for it. In the years to come I would work with some major headliners like Jake Johannsen, Darrell Hammond, Craig Ferguson, and more. I was a regular opener at the San Jose

Improv for a few years. I went on the road and worked weekends at smaller clubs. I even did a full week in the Midwest at the Funny Bone Comedy Club as the feature act.

Unfortunately, I was not able to support myself with the money I earned while performing stand-up. Unless you're at the top of the circuit, stand-up just doesn't pay well. I continued doing stand-up while I was working part-time. For the next few years, comedy was my priority. I still did every show I could, but it was hard to find the balance.

In the Fall of 2005, with the encouragement of my sister I thought I'd try substitute teaching. That way I could work part-time. Going back to work was challenging, but I was ready. More important, I started slowly. I taught two or three times per week and performed stand-up comedy on the side. Luckily, substitute teaching gave me a lot of material! And the shame of living with my sister and her husband was a constant theme of my comedy. Many of my sets would start, "So my comedy career is going so well, that I decided to take the next step … and move in with my sister and her husband." I learned to laugh at my difficult situation—most of the time.

In summer of 2006, a little over two years after my hospitalization and almost two years living with my sister, I got a temporary full-time job that allowed me to support myself and live on my own. It was near San Francisco, and I worked as a logistics coordinator at a summer camp. This job enabled me to move out of my sister's house and rent a room in a townhouse in the city near San Francisco State University. My two other housemates were journalism students at the same university.

After the summer job ended, I struggled to find a full-time job. I went back to substitute teaching while I looked for permanent work. I sent out what seemed like one hundred resumes and got back nothing. I barely even got an interview. At least while I was on disability earlier, I'd had time to research careers, and I saw a career counselor for additional help. As I'd always liked to teach, I realized that something related to education would be a better career path for me than business had been. It was tough changing career paths. I decided to take the leap.

I wanted to work at a nonprofit, hopefully one that dealt in some way with education. I knew I needed a job in a field that I believed in. Unfortunately, no employer would even consider me. Many jobs required a master's degree, and the fact that I hadn't worked full-time for two years didn't help my chances either. Each time I applied for work, I was confronted with a big, embarrassing gap in my work history. Trying to explain the gap by describing my time in the mental hospital didn't seem like a good idea.

I kept trying and kept getting the rejection letters. I was so frustrated. I felt as if all my years of college and work experience had been discounted and seemed so outdated.

I decided that my best option was to go back to school. I chose to go to San Francisco State University to get my masters in adult education. I didn't know exactly what type of work I would get when I was done, perhaps a job at an adult school or college, but I was excited to start my program. To me, adult education is so important. It's like a second chance at life. Many people think that you only go to school once and then you work for the rest of your life. I disagree: We should constantly be learning and growing, reinventing ourselves, like snakes shedding an old skin. Graduate school would give me a second chance to make a new career and new life. More important, I chose a field that could help others do the same.

I was able to get student loans to help pay for school and for my room and board. I went to school full-time and then worked at Peets Coffee & Tea part-time as a barista so I could get health benefits. I worked at the Peets in the heart of the Castro District, which was a great experience. I could write another whole book just on that! Although I loved making lattes for the fun and charming folks of the Castro, the crack-of-dawn hours were difficult for me.

After almost a year, I stopped working at Peets and started teaching English as a Second Language. I really enjoyed teaching and loved working with diverse students from various countries. I also got accepted into a program at SFSU that took a group of graduate students to China for two weeks to study the Chinese education system. It was an unforgettable experience. China is a beautiful country. Oddly enough, I did not like Chinese food in China. It tastes nothing like authentic Chinese food, you know, like the stuff you find at Panda Express.

After a year and a half, I finished graduate school. It was the beginning of 2009, and once again, I struggled to find a full-time job. I lived at home with my parents during the summers and taught ESL. Almost a year after I'd graduated, I finally got a full-time job with benefits.

More than five years later, I am still at this job. I am a program coordinator for a nonprofit educational organization that helps healthcare workers advance their careers. I wear many different hats at this job. I handle logistics, planning, billing and designing marketing materials. I also conduct outreach, doing things like visiting hospitals, speaking at union-steward council meetings and teaching people about their education benefits.

I am so grateful for this job. It allows me to help others create a life they may have dreamed about but thought was out of their reach. It gives people that second chance. In addition, unlike my job at the media research company, my current employer knows how to treat its workers. I work extremely hard at my job, but am able to stay emotionally and mentally stable. Most of the time. It may also help that I am in a union now, so I have rights. I have excellent benefits that give me access to great doctors and affordable medication. My manager is extremely understanding and is not bothered that I have to see a doctor, my psychiatrist, about every three weeks. I do good work in a healthy environment.

In 2010 I had to change doctors. Dr. Shoreman was too far away for me to see on a regular basis, so I started working with a new psychiatrist. I am lucky to have found an excellent one in Sacramento. He's an expert in the field of bipolar disorder and is constantly doing research into new treatment methods. He gives me all the information and then, with his guidance, allows me to choose the route I want to follow. He helps me see the big picture and helps me let go of my need to be perfect. Maybe more important, he's a nice guy. No teddy bears, but I still look forward to talking with him.

With my doctor's help, in 2010 I began to look at updating my medications. At that point I was only on Lithium and Wellbutrin. (I'd stopped taking Seroquel Immediate Release and Ambien about ten months after my hospitalization in 2004, tapering off of them with the help of Dr. Shoreman.) In fact, I had been on Wellbutrin and Lithium for seventeen years! I couldn't believe how long it had been. I was ready for a change. I didn't feel like Lithium was working well for me anymore. I seemed to have more anxiety than I felt was normal. In addition, Lithium's side effects are really rough, too. Nausea, dry skin, dry hair, acne; I had been going through those things for so long!

My psychiatrist suggested I try Seroquel Extended Release XR in place of the Lithium. It is different from the Seroquel I had used before because it stays in my system longer. It is a very popular drug used for bipolar disorder. So I thought about it and I took a chance. I slowly tapered off Lithium and started taking this new drug. I really liked how it made me feel! I am so grateful that I tried it. Yes, Lithium did help with mood swings, but this drug helped far more. My lows are not as low and my highs are not as high. Even on Lithium I struggled with depression. This new drug helps with depression and mania. I just want to add a disclaimer here. I don't want to promote Seroquel XR. I have only been on it a few years so I am not sure of the long-term effects.

Now and again I experience some mild mania. To be honest, it's hard to say what is mania and what is just getting excited. After a really good comedy show, I do get a little bit of a high, and it's hard to turn my mind off and go to sleep. The Seroquel helps slow down my brain. Sure, I don't get to live out the high all night long, but being healthy is more important. What the medication really helps the most with is the everyday, racing thoughts that can take over my brain. For me, mania has become less about the high and more about getting lost in my mind, in the overthinking that I can experience as my mind obsesses about a topic.

One of the big problems of Seroquel is the side effects. They're pretty strong. I gained weight at first. I could never get full. It was as if I had a bottomless stomach. I would eat three big bowls of cereal in the morning and be like, and what else? Oh, and talk about the "c" word—I'm not talking about crazy here. Let's just say that I have to be hyper-conscious of my fiber intake. It also makes me feel incredibly tired and drowsy, at night and in the morning.

In an attempt to lessen the side effects of my new medication, I decided I wanted to lower the dose by two-thirds. My doctor wasn't crazy about the idea, but helped me do it safely. If there was any doubt in my mind whether or not I need medication, it was put to rest when I tried this experiment. At first it seemed fine, but oh boy, did my life get rough.

I stayed on this low dosage for six months. Six terrible months. My anxiety went out of control. I had fits of rage at my boyfriend. I almost had a nervous breakdown one weekend because the house was messy. My emotions seemed to take over, no matter how irrational they were. I was able to hide this from the outside world, but my poor boyfriend got the brunt of it. It wasn't like I wasn't working on my emotions or myself. I was meditating and taking care of myself as I normally did. I finally decided to go back to my usual dosage of the medication. In fact, the idea to go back to that dosage came to me while meditating. Just a few weeks back on the right dose and presto-chango, life got a whole lot better. I still have anxiety, but not nearly as bad.

I decided I needed to simply deal with the side effects. I didn't want to go back on Lithium. I know that some side effects can go away over time, or that you can get used to them. I went to the gym more often and learned what foods made me gain weight. I am still about five to ten pounds heavier than I was before I started the Seroquel XR, but, oh well. I discovered the best times to take my medications to reduce the drowsiness. As for the big "c"—well, that's a constant battle. But I am trying to have a sense of humor about it.

I wish I could say that I am totally over the side effects of both meds I am on, but I am not. The reality is, they really are tough. I also have to think about the long-term consequences of meds. For example, the Lithium damaged my thyroid. I will always have to take meds for that. Being on my psych meds causes dry mouth. Because of that I have had many cavities, no matter how hard I try to avoid them. I floss twice a day, have dramatically cut back sugar, use a water floss, and use prescription toothpaste. I had weird stomach issues a year ago that may or may not have to do with my meds. Despite all this I have to look at the big picture. Me being stable, happy, and mentally healthy trumps them all. I choose to have a stable life, which means I have to deal with the side effects of medication until we discover a better way to treat mental illness.

Since I am taking medications I try really, really hard to eat healthily and use natural preventive measures. I have become obsessed with nutrition and clean eating. As I mentioned, I cut out sugar dramatically. Daily I eat a ton of vegetables and a scoop of green powder that has spiralina and other nutrients. I get the omega-whatevers. I take probiotics. I drink water all day. I have seen many naturopathic doctors, as well as chiropractors and acupuncturists. Unfortunately, many of them, no joke, have been rather rude and mean to me once they hear I am on medications. Several have told me that I needed to go off "that poison." However, they have no idea what I have been through. They have no idea what it feels like to lose your mind and sense of reality. So I have to find the nice ones who accept Western medicine. I believe that natural alternative medicine can work in conjunction with Western medicine. It doesn't have to be one or the other. Can't we just all get along?

I have developed a routine that works for me if I stick with it consistently. I take my medications regularly. I meditate every day. I eat balanced and nutritious meals. I exercise regularly. I go on walks. I journal. As I mentioned, I include alternative medicine, like chiropractic and acupuncture. I make sure I get enough sleep. I make time for creative projects. I need creativity to remain stable. If I don't have something creative to work on, whether it is stand-up, writing, preparing a speech, or making a video, I can get kind of depressed. Creativity is my saving grace, and is more powerful than difficult emotions. I make my creative projects a priority. Most important, I am working on being nice to myself, letting go of the perfectionism.

I still struggle at times, just like everyone else. To be honest, I almost lost it at several times writing this book! It was very ironic. I felt like I was going crazy while trying to write a book about how I went crazy. Finding adequate time for my work, my stand-up, this book project, and my personal life is/was incredibly challenging. But I am learning a lot about patience and balance. Working full-time is no small task, and with all of the other things that I am committed to doing in my life, I could easily be going 24/7. I need, I absolutely need, to take time for myself and get enough sleep. That's a decision that I think too many of us don't make.

As I'm getting older, I'm starting to recognize negative emotions more quickly. But now, instead of trying to fix the bad moods, I just try to ride them out. It's like riding out a storm. You can't stop it, so just get to a safe place and know that it will soon be over. I still get depressed and a little manic, but the bouts are much fewer and farther between.

Unfortunately, since I've been able to get a handle on the mania and depression of my illness, anxiety has been showing up even more. In the last five years, I've started to experience some obsessive-compulsive symptoms. OCD has become an unexpected guest that has stayed longer than I would like it to. I have a hard time leaving my house sometimes. I check and recheck the lock on the door, as well as making sure that all burners and appliances are turned off. I sometimes get the "what if" worries: "what if *this* happens, and what if *that* happens?" I am working with my doctor on these. It's an ongoing process, and my medications and healthy choices are helping. I am, happily, treating this issue without judging myself. That may be my second book. Stay tuned.

Books, television shows and movies about positive thinking are a big part of my life. Oprah's *Super Soul Sunday* shows have been so incredibly helpful in my journey to wellness. I am a big fan of her and her guests; they are people who help us see the big picture and inspire us to find ways to connect to something bigger than ourselves. They help me work on my mindset and focus on my goals.

Another reason for my recovery is *who* I have chosen to be in my life. My family and friends are incredibly supportive and positive. I try not to have any toxic relationships that will bring me down. I think we all know who these people are. Most important, I have a wonderful man in my life. He is so loving, and is accepting of who I truly am. I am very happy with him, and we are growing together. We see our life as a journey, and we have so many things to look forward to.

Oh, and as for the chocolate pudding ... you didn't think I would put it in the title without bringing it back into the story, did you? The heavenly magic of the chocolate pudding I savored at the hospital during my third episode has returned to my life. I eat it almost every day and enjoy every delectable bite. However, it's not that chemical-filled, chocolate-flavored goo that I circled on the dinner menu. I invented a new pudding that fits my nutritional priorities. My boyfriend thinks it's weird, but I love it. I take plain Greek yogurt (none of that flavored yogurt with the sugar), a banana, real cocoa powder (the kind that doesn't have any sugar), and many spoonfuls of peanut butter, and mix with an electric immersion hand blender. The banana sweetens the yogurt and the cocoa. It is awesome! I love it. It's almost heavenly.

Basically, I have recovered from my last episode and I am constantly working on maintaining the stability that I desired. I created a new life with a career that was less stressful and I stuck with a rigorous treatment plan. I am profoundly grateful for the loving care offered by those closest to me, and for the professional care given by those in the places where I was hospitalized. I guess you could say that I am in crazy remission.

One of my greatest joys throughout all of it has been doing stand-up. Stand-up comedy has a way of forcing me to look at things differently, from a unique perspective. Stand-up is the place where I first started to accept who I was. It is the place where I fit in, and, perhaps paradoxically, the place where I am most grateful for my differences. On stage I am not a mental patient—I'm just me.

I have had to cut back on doing comedy for the past few years as I wrote this book. Although I love the financial stability of working full-time, it doesn't leave a lot of time for much else. Every year since I began my current full-time job, I've done comedy less and less. So I have only done about two to three shows each year. Someday I hope to return to the mic when I have time to write new jokes and get stage time to practice. I don't think it's possible to fully run out of embarrassing moments or absurd situations, so I know I'll have lots of material still left to share.

In the meantime, I have felt something tugging at my insides. Just like I wanted to write my story down ever since I was sixteen, I have been feeling more and more like I want to share it with people in person. Writing it all down for the first time was like coming out. Here I am warts and all. Now I would like to take my story on the road. I am already starting to speak in public about my experience with mental illness. I would love, as time goes on, to incorporate a bit of humor, a bit of comedy, into my speeches. It will be a little like bringing together two worlds. I hope that maybe sharing my story will help others see mental illness differently. It's not always what you think. I am not alone in this journey. There are many others like me just trying to live a normal life. Perhaps if society can be compassionate toward people who are suffering from mental illness rather than judge them, it will make a profound difference.

In my recovery, in my crazy remission, maybe the best thing I have accomplished is that I am learning to let go of the shame and the guilt. I am able to fully accept who I am, and that has made the act of living so much sweeter … just like chocolate pudding.

# living in god's waiting room

So, over ten years have passed since my last episode and over twenty years since my first. Wow, time flies—when you put it in a book and make a story out of it. Thank you for listening. I can't believe how far I have come. Does my recovery mean I won't encounter hard times? Absolutely not. As I mentioned, I still have really tough days when my emotions take me hostage. Moreover, it is possible that I will become manic or experience clinical depression again. But I will keep going, treating my highs and lows the best I can. I think it's important to welcome both the good and the bad. Through this acceptance it is easier to continue moving in the direction of good. I will never be "cured." And I don't want to be. I like who I am. I just need to work on managing the negative symptoms of this illness. As clichéd as it sounds, I see my life as a journey and not a destination. I have a long road ahead of me, but I take it day by day. Luckily, I have developed a pretty effective routine.

My weekday mornings are a good example.

My first alarm goes off on my personal cell phone at 6:15 am, and I hit the snooze immediately. I feel so sleepy, like I am just waking up from a coma. "No!" I think to myself, "Need more sleep!" Part of the grogginess is due to the medication and part of it is because I probably should have gone to bed earlier. "Damn you, Maggie-from-last-night," I think to myself. I press the snooze button about four times until it is almost 7:00 am. This is when I must get up if I want to get to work on time. In case I decide to pitch my personal cell phone out the window, my work cell phone alarm goes off as well. I try to turn it off swiftly, but end up knocking both phones off my bedside table, making a huge ruckus.

I have heard it's bad to keep cell phones, especially work phones, in your bedroom. Something about bad energy. But I tempt fate and keep them both on my nightstand.

Fortunately, I didn't wake up my boyfriend (yes, I have been living in sin with my boyfriend for three years). I look over at him. He is sound asleep, breathing loudly with his mouth open like a dead fish, a rather cute dead fish if I do say so.

I stumble out of the bedroom. Our cat, Sadie, is waiting outside our door and gives me a mournful meow, like the world is going to end. In case I missed it, she meows again, and again. "Okay, okay," I say. "Hold on." She wants me to turn the bathtub water on. This little prima donna will only drink water when it drips out of the bathtub. I pick her up and give her a little kiss on her nose. My dad always used to say to me, "Don't kiss the cat. The cat's dirty." I am an adult, however, and I do what I want.

After I put her in the tub, I go to the sink and look at myself in the mirror. I see a tired face, my hair is all over the place, but my eyes still have a sparkle. I go into the kitchen and immediately start to make breakfast. I am starving, as per usual! I make oatmeal, add a little coconut oil, cinnamon, blueberries, and nuts. Dr. Oz would be proud of me. I quickly eat my oatmeal. It doesn't totally fill me up, but that will have to do for now.

I go to my medicine cupboard. Some people have a modest medicine chest in their bathroom; I have a huge medicine cupboard in my kitchen. I go to my premade pill case and take out a fistful of pills. There's my thyroid meds and my Wellbutrin that I must take. Then I have some other supplements: Vitamin D (because my last blood test showed I am deficient in it), Vitamin C (so I don't get sick), a stool softener (for, well, you know) and fish oil (for those omega-whatevers). I almost take calcium, but then remember my doctor told me I can't take it with my thyroid meds. Man, so much to remember. I also take my birth control pill, which, on a political note, I would need to take even if I weren't in a relationship because it regulates my cycle. Then I go to my freezer and take out the green yuck-yuck stuff. That isn't really the name, but that's what it tastes like. It's natural greens in a powder, spirulina, wheatgrass, you name it. It's got all the good stuff—at least that's what it says. But man oh man, is it disgusting. I put a scoop in some water, stir it, then hold my breath and drink it down. Just get it over with, I say. I also take a probiotic from my refrigerator. Okay, done with all pills until nighttime, when I take my other psych med and that calcium.

Now it's time for my meditation, or at least my attempt at it. I lie down in our spare room. I set my timer for five minutes. I would love to do twenty minutes straight, but I always fall asleep, so I do this. The first two sets I chant "Ah-h-h-h-h. Ah-h-h-h-h" and the last two sets I chant "Om-m-m-m. Om-m-m-m." I'm not an expert, but I think I heard that Ahh and Om means God, or whatever name someone has for the Divine. I want to quiet my mind. So with every set of Ahh or Om chants, I try to think about nothing. I try to connect to that peaceful, strong, loving and wise part of me that I believe is connected with God. Some days I don't fee like chanting so I just do a silent meditation. It brings me peace, but many times my mind wanders. What will I wear today? What will the weather be like? Why did women wear shoulder pads in the 80s? I try to get myself back to the calm. Sometimes I can do it, sometimes I can't. I keep trying.

When I'm done, I rush to get dressed. I pick out some green corduroy pants and a nice blouse from my closet. I head to the laundry room and rummage through the unmatched socks for a match. Someday I will finally find all the matches and put them away.

Today I will be opening up a computer class that I've organized for healthcare workers. A nervous pang hits my stomach. What if the teacher doesn't show up? That would be awful. Then I remember what I've been working on with my doctor. I don't know what is going to happen. And if he doesn't show up, I can handle it. Focus on now, I tell myself.

I look at the clock. I am on schedule, and it's time for what may be my favorite part of my day. I quickly make my special chocolate pudding. I throw the yogurt, peanut butter, banana, and cacao powder into a bowl. I mix it up with an electric immersion hand blender, and voila, it is my dessert for breakfast! Since I cut out sugar dramatically, I have to make sure that I don't have cravings all day. So I get to have my healthy version of a dessert every morning. It is my special time. I sample my creation. It's perfect. I take the bowl, walk into the living room, and sit on my couch.

I instantly see my boyfriend's old socks and shoes on the ground, as well as some snacks on the coffee table from the night before that he didn't put away. Ugh, I think. I can't stand messes or clutter. I take a deep breath. I let it go. I know I am guilty sometimes of doing the same.

I look over and see Sadie on the chair. Her leg is in the air and her head is down … well, let's say she is cleaning herself. Okay, let's be honest, she's licking her butt. Then she looks up at me and licks her lips. Aw, man. I immediately regret kissing her. I contemplate going to the bathroom and rinsing my mouth out with Scope. But it's too late. Damage done. Maybe dad was right.

The sun has lit up our modest living room. A picture framed of me when I was about six years old and sitting with my dad catches my attention. I see that little girl, that superstar, so happy, so carefree. I smile, as if I am connecting with an old friend. She is still with me. I will *never* let her go.

Then I look over and see a picture of me on stage, doing stand-up. Wow, I don't even recognize myself. This Maggie is so cool and confident. I miss her. I know I will be back on stage again soon. Maybe it will be at a comedy show, or maybe I will be speaking to a group of psychiatrists. I have my first joke already lined up.

Finally, my eyes land on a picture of me, with my boyfriend and my friends. I feel so grateful for that one. How lucky am I? I think to myself.

The room is quiet. I have just a few more minutes to soak in the peace before I have to go to work. I pick up my special chocolate pudding. I scoop up a spoonful and take a bite of the creamy, chocolaty delight. The texture and flavor are just perfect. I savor every bite, then dive back in for more. It tastes amazing. I look around the room again. I take a deep peaceful breath.

I have come home, and I am safe.

# postscript

So why did I write this book now? I couldn't hold it in anymore. Twenty years was long enough. I was tired of having this big secret. I have wanted to write about my manic experiences ever since I had the first one at the age of sixteen, but I didn't have enough understanding about what happened to me until now. And I was so full of guilt and so filled with shame for so many years that I abandoned every attempt to tell my story. I also needed to get the timing right. I needed to be sure that I was stable and at peace with myself before I told my story. It has taken me twenty years to get to this place, but at last I am here.

Most important, I have written this book because I think that now, more than ever, we need to open an honest dialogue about mental illness. Every day in the news it seems like we see the repercussions of untreated mental illness.

As I mentioned in the beginning, in America, it's estimated that 26.3 % of people over the age of 18 suffer from mental illness, or *one out of every four adults.* And these are only the people who are diagnosed! Just to put this in perspective: at the time of this writing, the number of Americans who have cancer is currently over 14 million. But nearly *43.7 million Americans* experience a mental health condition *every year.*

Clearly, there's a problem here, a big problem. As a 2010 article in *Scientific American* said, "Mental health care is one of the biggest unmet needs of our time," and "Young people are especially prone to these troubles."

The problem of unaddressed mental illness is bad for the country. According to the World Health Organization, mental disorders are the leading cause of disability in the U.S. and Canada. And, according to the National Alliance on Mental Illness, "Untreated mental illnesses in the U.S. cost more than $100 billion a year in lost productivity." The workplace isn't the only place that's affected, either. Hospitals, clinics, courts, and jails must, every day, deal with the chronic physical diseases that often accompany untreated mental illness, and if the person suffering doesn't have insurance, the cost for this treatment skyrockets.

Perhaps the cruelest losses are the deaths. Quoting again from that recent article in *Scientific American*, "Suicide ranks among the top 15 most common killers in the U.S. (in the top three among young people), and 90 percent of cases can be attributed to mental illness." Every year, in America alone, hundreds of lives are lost, thousands of dollars are lost, and millions are affected—and all by something that many won't discuss and much less address.

When people don't get help, they find other ways to deal with it. Many often turn to alcohol or drugs and then often come to believe that these substances are the cause of the pain. Their substance abuse is, however, just a symptom of the larger issue. It is a coping mechanism to deal with the heartbreaking emotions that often come from a mental illness. We see it too often: talented people ending their lives by overdosing on drugs and alcohol.

Although efforts have been made in recent years to provide education and attempt to de-stigmatize mental illness, we are still completely rejecting many members of our society who suffer from this condition. We fall into judgment, we succumb to jokes and name-calling. We ignore the problem, we resist getting involved and we isolate those who we feel are too "out there." All of these things do their part to stop people from getting help. I think it starts with compassion and accepting people where they are.

With this book I would also like to heighten people's awareness of society's tendency to use mental illness as a way of labeling people. Mental illness defines, for most people, a person's identity, rather than being seen as a condition a person is dealing with. I would like society to start to see that mental illness is not an issue that can be defined by black-and-white thinking. Many of us are still more comfortable with things that are absolute rather than things that are nuanced: countries are either good or evil, actions either right or wrong, and a person is either cool or a loser. Many people's mindsets regarding mental illness tend to fall into this same mode of thinking. Although each of the approximately twenty types of mental illness displays extremely different symptoms, our society has historically blurred the lines between them. It has lumped all forms of mental illness together and given all those who have them one name—crazy. You are either crazy or you are sane. Either nuts or normal. Mental illness should be seen as less of a black-or-white absolute and more of a condition that ebbs and flows according to a person's genetics, moods and current situation.

If you think about it, we are all dealing with challenges. Whether it's a mental illness, relationship problem, financial crisis, physical impairment, or any other challenge, we all struggle. It's part of being human. Whether we can admit it or not, we are *all* a little crazy. There is no normal. Some of us, like me, need more help in dealing with the crazy. My "crazy" stopped me from living the life I wanted. Once I accepted it, owned it, and worked with it, I found a life full of stability and joy.

Another way that society can start seeing the *person* rather than the *illness* is to understand that untreated mental disorders are actually physical illnesses, a chemical imbalance in the brain. I see mental illness as a brain disorder, as a physical illness no different than diabetes or heart problems. Like these illnesses, mental illness is caused by a combination of genetic predisposition and environment. For diabetes and heart problems, medication is often required, and we do not pass judgment on those who use it. They are encouraged to get treatment because we know that modern medicine, as well as diet and lifestyle modifications, dramatically improves these conditions. The same could be said for mental illness, but most people who need help avoid treatment. This may be because once someone gets any sort of mental health treatment, it is automatically perceived that something is wrong with that person. He doesn't want to be seen as "crazy." He is embarrassed and ashamed.

If you take anything from this book, I hope that you are a little more empathetic for those dealing with mental illness and know that mental illness is not a personality or a choice, but an illness that can be treated. As I mentioned, treating a mental illness can be incredibly difficult and lonely, but totally worth it. Staying on my mental health treatment all these years is the hardest thing that I have ever done.

If you have an illness, don't be afraid to ask for help. Be patient with yourself. Accepting an illness and finding treatment is a long process. If you know someone that has an illness, your non-judgmental support and patience could really help make the difference. See more in the upcoming section "Advice For Treatment" and my website at www.maggienewcomb.com.

When I close my eyes and envision the world I long for, we are opening our hearts and opening the doors for those who suffer. We are allocating more resources and funding for diagnostic support and treatment. We have an opportunity to create a healthy society of people who are no longer ashamed of who they are. To do so, we need to vigorously address the issue of mental illness. However, we can do so in a way that is kind and loving and devoid of prejudice and judgment. I am not saying that we have to hold hands and sing *Kumbaya*. Let's accept the reality and do something about it.

I am coming out now for a number of reasons, but the main one is the hope that this book will help change our perspective on mental illness. Now, my intention is to speak in public about mental illness as often as I am asked and am able to do so. I am a mental health advocate and activist. I have a unique perspective about mental illness that is hopefully positive, entertaining, and inspiring. Every time I hear of another shooting or suicide, I get this pain in my stomach. If that person had known how to treat his or her mental illness, would this have happened? I don't know for sure, but I do know there are so many people suffering who can be helped.

I will do whatever it takes for the rest of my life to share my story, and, more importantly, to share my message. It is a message of acceptance, education, compassion and action. I want to be part of the change that can not only save lives but improve the quality of life for all.

Will you join me?

*part 3* | ADVICE FOR
         TREATMENT

# emergency info

If you are in a crisis and are thinking of hurting yourself or others, don't wait! ACT NOW!

- Call your doctor's office (if you have one).
- Call 911 for emergency services.
- If you are able to, go to the nearest hospital emergency room.
- Call the National Suicide Prevention Lifeline at 1-800-273-TALK (1-800-273-8255). They are open 24 hours each day and will connect you to a trained counselor at their closest available suicide crisis center.
- Call the National HOPEline Network at 1-800-442-HOPE (4673) or 1-800-SUICIDE to speak with someone immediately. They offer a number of crisis hotlines, including ones for veterans, teens, Spanish-speaking people, grad students and those suffering from postpartum depression.

# resources

- National Institute for Mental Health – www.nimh.nih.gov – 1-866-615-6464 1-866-415-8051 (TTY)
- National Alliance for Mental Illness – www.nami.org – 800-950-6264
- Mental Health.Gov – www.mentalhealth.gov – 1-877-696-6775
- American Psychiatric Foundation – www.psych.org – 1-888 35-PSYCH, Ext. 3
- Depression and Bipolar Support Alliance – www.dbsalliance. org – 800-826-3632
- Mental Health First Aid – www.mentalhealthfirstaid.org
- My website – maggienewcomb.com

# getting help

When you're suffering from a mental illness, it can be hard to know where to begin. It's often much easier to try to ignore what's happening in your life than it is to accept the illness and decide to start treating it. No matter what your mental challenges or emotional struggles are, they do not have to rule your life. You *can* recover from them.

Asking for help is not a sign of weakness; it is a sign of strength. It takes courage to realize that there are aspects of your life that aren't working. It takes courage to accept that you're not happy. It takes courage to decide that you deserve a better life. It takes courage to get help. Pick up a phone, go online, talk to someone. Then congratulate yourself. Acceptance is the first step.

The second step is finding a good doctor and treatment plan. There are many great doctors out there. If you can afford one or have insurance, start looking for a psychiatrist. Don't be afraid to meet with different doctors before you choose one. Remember, you want to work with someone you're comfortable with, and who has the same goals as you do. If you don't have insurance, go to HealthCare.gov online or call them at 1-800-318-2596 to find low-cost coverage in your area.

Another great place to start is NAMI (National Alliance on Mental Illness). Visit them at www.nami.org to learn about what they do. Then click onto the "Support and Program" icon on the top menu to find out more. If you don't have access to a computer, call their Information Helpline at 1-800-950-NAMI. Nearly all local chapters have support groups and classes where you can learn more about the illness and its treatment options, and contact information for organizations that can help you. Everything that NAMI offers is free of charge.

Never, never be ashamed of who you are. Don't try to "fix" yourself because there is nothing wrong with you. Just do whatever you can, in whatever way you can, to manage your condition and achieve long-term stability. Depression, mania, and anxiety *are* manageable. You do not have to suffer with them. Having a mental illness is not a choice. However, treating the illness is a choice. The life you want to experience is your choice, and doing what needs to be done to create that experience is also your choice. No matter how difficult your situation is, know this: you have the power to create who you are.

As you journey out into the world each day, look for the "you" who is buried underneath all those emotions. Who is that person? What does he want? What makes her happy? Invest in yourself. It's never too late. It's never impossible. The time to make positive changes in your life is now. No matter what, do not give up. Do not give up. Do not give up. The life you want is waiting for you

# tips for recovery and lifelong stability

I know it can be hard to ask for help. I know it can be really difficult to take the steps that will help you recover. I promise you that both of these things are worth it.

Here are some of the major actions and attitudes that helped me recover from my mental illness:

1. Believe that recovery is possible, and that you deserve to have a life that you enjoy.
2. Get health insurance or Medicaid.
3. Take time to find a doctor who is right for you.
4. Be open to the idea of a treatment plan that may include medication.
5. Don't be afraid to ask family and friends for help, or to tell them how they can best help you. Contact organizations for no-cost or low-cost support and for information on resources.
6. Stick with your treatment plan and do not go off your medication. Give the meds enough time to fully work. Talk to your doctor if you want to try others.
7. Give yourself as much time as possible to recover.

8. Accept the responsibility of your illness, and commit fully to its treatment.

9. Know that you are not your illness. Your illness is something you treat.

10. Keep focusing on the kind of life you want to have, not what you don't have.

11. Find or develop a hobby or activity in your life that brings you joy and gives you something to live for (art, dancing, gardening, acting. Stand-up comedy, bungee-jumping, power-knitting, robot-building, whatever).

12. Incorporate alternative methods of treatment, like chiropractic and acupuncture.

13. Get creative with your treatment. Try music and journaling to get through the tough times.

14. Work at quieting your mind. Meditate daily, and be grateful for your life.

15. Learn about nutrition and eat healthily. Consider incorporating some nutritional supplements into your diet, as appropriate.

16. Exercise regularly, even if it is just walking.

17. See your experience with mental illness as a journey and not a destination.

18. Don't give up. No matter how hard things get, *know* that they will get better.

19. Don't give up.

20. I mean it, don't give up.

21. Did I mention not to give up?

22. Seriously, don't give up.

23. In case you thought I was kidding about giving up, I'm not. So don't do it.

24. Don't you dare ever give up!

25. No te rindas! (That's Spanish for don't give up.)

# supporting a loved one with mental illness

One of the hardest parts of about mental illness is watching someone you love suffer through it. You probably feel helpless and frustrated. Although you can't make the illness go away or do the work for your loved one, there are things that you can do to help someone. This could be an entire book on its own. For every kind relationship there is a different level of support. The appropriate support of a parent, spouse, boyfriend or caregiver will look completely different from the support of a friend or co-workers. There is no one-size-fits-all support plan.

I highly recommend taking a great course called Mental Health First Aid. This is an 8-hour course that teaches you how to help someone who is developing a mental health problem or experiencing a mental health crisis. The training helps you identify, understand, and respond to signs of addictions and mental illnesses. I can't recommend this class enough. And, it is offered free to the public. Go to www.mentalhealthfirstaid.org. If you don't have time to take the class, you can buy their book.

Some general tips that I would give are to encourage your loved one to work with a mental health specialist, psychiatrist or therapist.

Tell them that you are there to support them. Listen to them non-judgmentally. Do not try to treat them; you are not their doctor. I think it's best to straight out ask them, "How can I support you?" Educate yourself on the illness. There is a lot of information out there now about mental illness. Get some background knowledge of the condition from experts. Maybe encourage your loved one to read more about it. Know it is not your responsibility to "fix" them. Mental health treatment can be a lifelong journey. You can just be another positive person in their lives guiding them in the right direction.

For more information on how to support your loved ones, go to my website at www.maggienewcomb.com.

# references

## Scared to Come Out

"From Discovery to Cure: Accelerating the Development of New and Personalized Interventions for Mental Illnesses: Report of the National Advisory Mental Health Council's Workgroup," *National Institute of Mental Health,* August, 2010, http://www. nimh.nih.gov/about/advisory-boards-and-groups/namhc/reports/ fromdiscoverytocure_103739.pdf

"Mental Illnesses: What is Mental Illness?" *National Alliance of Mental Illness,* http://www2.nami.org/Template.cfm?Section=By_Illness&templ

"Director's Update: Mental Disorders as Brain Disorders: Thomas Insel at TEDxCaltech," *National Institute of Mental Health,* http:// www.nimh.nih.gov/about/updates/2013/mental-disorders-as-brain- disorders-thomas-insel-at-tedxcaltech.shtml

"People with Mental Illness Enrich Our Lives," *National Alliance of Mental Illness,* http://www.nami.org/Template.cfm?Section=Helpline1&template=/ ContentManagement/ContentDisplay.cfm&ContentID=4858

## The Diagnosis

"Health and Education: Bipolar Disorder: What Is Bipolar Disorder?" *National Institute of Mental Health*, http://www.nimh.nih.gov/health/topics/bipolar-disorder/index.shtml

"Bipolar Disorder: Symptoms, Causes and Diagnosis," *National Alliance of Mental Illness*, http://www.nami.org/Learn-More/Mental-Health-Conditions/Bipolar-Disorder

"Criteria for Manic Episode: DSM-5," *National Alliance of Mental Illness*, http://www2.nami.org/Content/NavigationMenu/Intranet/Homefront/Criteria_Manic_Episode.pdf

## Lurking Depression

Pearl, June 16, 2010 comment on "Exploring the Links between Depression and Weight Gain," Roni Caryn Rabin, *New York Times, Well column,* http://well.blogs.nytimes.com/2010/06/16/exploring-the-links-between-depression-and-weight-gain/comment-page-2/#respond

## Postscript

"Cancer Treatment & Survivorship Facts & Figures," *The American Cancer Society*, http://www.cancer.org/research/cancerfactsstatistics/survivor-facts-figures

"Mental Health by the Numbers," *National Alliance on Mental Illness*, http://www.nami.org/Learn-More/Mental-Health-By-the-Numbers

"The Neglect of Mental Illness Exacts a Huge Toll, Human and Economic," Editors, *Scientific American* 306, no. 3, March 1, 2012, http://www.scientificamerican.com/article/a-neglect-of-mental-illness

"Mental Health and Mental Disorders," *Office of Disease Prevention and Health Promotion*, http://www.healthypeople.gov/2020/topics-objectives/topic/mental-health-and-mental-disorders

"Leaders Criticize Threatened Mental Health Service Budget Cuts, Call for Statewide Plan, West Virginia is First State in New National Campaign," *National Alliance on Mental Illness*, Media Advisory for Monday, January 26, 2004, http://www.nami.org/Template.cfm?Section=court_watch1&template=/ContentManagement/ContentDisplay.cfm&ContentID=85717

CPSIA information can be obtained
at www.ICGtesting.com
Printed in the USA
BVHW080124140620
581354BV00002B/88